40TH ANNIVERSARY

WOODSTOCK

Peace, Music & Memories

Published by

700 East State Street • Iola, WI 54990-0001
715-445-2214 • 888-457-2873
www.krausebooks.com

Our toll-free number to place an order or obtain a free catalog is (800) 258-0929.

Library of Congress Control Number: 2008937696

ISBN-13: 978-0-89689-833-2
ISBN-10: 0-89689-833-4

Designed by Rachael Knier
Edited by Mary Sieber

Printed in China

On our cover

Front cover: Janis Joplin, photo courtesy Don Aters; Moonfire, photo courtesy John De Lorenzo; "Light" bus, photo courtesy Dr. Bob Hieronimus; Jimi Hendrix, photo courtesy David Marks (3rd Ear Music/Hidden Years Music Archives 1969-2009); and three-day advance pass to Woodstock. Back cover: Woodstock poster, photo courtesy Heritage Auction Galleries; and Woodstock at its height, photo courtesy Cornelius Alexy.

40TH ANNIVERSARY

WOODSTOCK

Peace, Music & Memories

Brad Littleproud and Joanne Hague

© Lisa Law Archives 1969

DEDICATION

We dedicate this book to
Mary-Lou Littleproud and Joseph Hague
and to our families for their time, patience and support to allow us to succeed—
now, in the past, and in the future.

CONTENTS

FOREWORD

It's been 40 years since half a million people gathered on Max Yasgur's farm, yet each anniversary is like a celebration of that night when Michael Lang and I dreamed the idea of what would become "Woodstock." I thought it important to keep alive the memories of the 1969 Woodstock festival, and I thank you, Brad and Joanne, for this book. Though it's true that Woodstock is a state of mind and not necessarily a place, it was for many the birthplace of a generation.

The Woodstock generation was comprised of war babies, and we were rock and roll babies. We lived in a time of great change, great promise, great violence and great despair—all happening simultaneously—and as young people we were searching for something. My good friend and wonderful artist, the late Bert Sommer, picked up on the vibe and sang what Paul Simon said was the best cover of any of his songs, "We've All Come to Look for America," and at Woodstock that's what everyone did. Woodstock was more than a concert. It was about issues concerning Vietnam, social changes, and ideals that no president or speech writer could touch. It was about caring for each other. It was about our generation.

People ask, "Whatever happened to the Woodstock generation?" to which I answer, "Well, we're still here." Though some of us have become complacent in the world and maybe a bit too comfortable, some of us continue to believe that there is much unfinished business left. The greatest hope I get is from those who have contacted me over the past 10 years. Not the 65-year-old hippies still lighting their hash pipes, but the 14- to 24-year-olds who ask what it was like to live in America during the 1960s, during the birth of rock and roll, and what it's like to be the "Father of Woodstock." You can hear the same sort of passion in their voices, expressing a feeling of love and concern for our planet and each other that I felt back in '69. The world is different now, yet the same as it was then, if you know what I mean: an environment we continue to abuse, a war that nobody wants. There's the same yearning for change in their voices—peace without violence. You can hear it in the new music. It's resurgence—protest songs about the desire for things to be better. These ideals are still alive, which gives me hope for our future. For the Woodstock generation, the only thing against us is our age, but we're still a force to be reckoned with and continue to fight for what we believe is right.

I'm proud that as co-creator and promoter of Woodstock, I was responsible for originally getting people to Yasgur's farm in a certain state of mind and giving them a festival that *was* their state of mind. Could there ever be another Woodstock? Never. It was a time and place in history that can't be repeated. We can certainly show that we care about one another, if we have the will, but Woodstock itself will forever remain as memories by those who shared that muddy hill with me and with each other, 40 years ago. I look for this book to take me back to a wonderful place and time I spent with half a million of my closest friends. To be at Woodstock meant you were in the mud, and that mud was like heavenly water washing away all that was wrong with the world at that time.

And when people ask me where Woodstock came from, I say, "From you. You're the people who gave me Woodstock. You gave me a great show."

Love, peace and music,
Artie Kornfeld
Co-creator and promoter, Woodstock '69

ACKNOWLEDGEMENTS

To create *Woodstock: Peace, Music & Memories* from a concept to a living account of this great event, it was necessary that all the material contained within this book come from those who were there—those who experienced Woodstock firsthand and/or understood its significance.

With sincere appreciation, we specifically acknowledge those who gave permission to use their own works, which provided essential historical context, content, and personal accounts.

MICHAEL WM. DOYLE, PH.D.

Associate Professor and Director, Public History Internship Program, Ball State University, Muncie, Indiana, and author of *The Statement on the Cultural and Historical Significance of the 1969 Woodstock Festival Site.*

STU FOX

Excerpts from "Song and Celebration." Published in the *Ithaca Times*, July 22, 1999.

ELLIOT TIBER

Excerpts from "How Woodstock Happened," with permission from *The Times-Herald Record* and Elliot Tiber. Text © 1994 *The Times-Herald-Record.*

THE TIMES-HERALD-RECORD

Middletown, New York, for permission to reprint various newspaper articles in this book.

THE WOODSTOCK-PRESERVATION ARCHIVES

www.woodstockpreservation.org
Timothy Dicks, Website Creator/Administrator

We are grateful for the support and enthusiasm of many people and especially extend our sincerest gratitude to everyone who helped bring this book to life by contributing their personal stories, experiences, photographs, and 8mm films to this project:

(In alphabetical order)
Jeryl Abramson
Cornelius Alexy (www.peacefence.com)
Don Aters (www.haightstreetmusicnews.com)
Clay Borris (www.johnphillipsphotography.com)
Babette Brackett
Tom Brady
Jim & Linda (Goldblatt) Breslin
Paul Campbell
Francis Cardamone
Robin Chanin
Christopher Cole (author of "The Closer's Song")
Peter J. Corrigan (www.vintagerockandrollphotos.com)
Richard Cutler
John De Lorenzo
Chuck Early
Nick and Bobbi (Kelly) Ercoline
Rosemary Forrest
Alan Futrell
Gary Geyer
Goldmine Magazine
Wavy Gravy (www.wavygravy.net)
Bob Grimm
Tommy Hayes (aka Tommy "Purple" Hayes)
Greg Henry
Dr. Bob Hieronimus
Dennis Himes
Larry Houman
Roy Howard
Patrick Howe
Elliott Landy (www.landyvision.com)

Chris Langhart

Michael Launder

Lisa Law (www.flashingonthesixties.com)

Paul Lehrman (for excerpts from "Out of the Garden," *Mix Magazine* [Penton Publishing], and *The Insider Audio Bathroom Reader* [Thomson Course PTR])

Lee Levin-Friend

Lynden Lilley

Leo Lyons (www.leolyons.org), bass player for Ten Years After

Victor Kahn (www.thegreatillusion.com)

Rich Klein

Artie Kornfeld (www.ArtieKornfeld-Woodstock.com)

Martie Malaker

David Marks (3rd Ear Music/Hidden Years Music Archives 1969-2009)

Trudy Morgal

Doug Mowrey

Scott A. Munroe

Donald Murphy

Nancy Nevins (www.NancyNevins.com), lead singer of Sweetwater

Jean Nichols (aka O2, Oxygen)

C. Duane Noto

Paul Novak

Derek Redmond

Jahanara Romney (www.campwinnarainbow.org), Director of Camp Winnarainbow

John Rossi

Caleb Rossiter (for excerpts from *The Chimes of Freedom Flashing: A Personal History of the Vietnam Anti-War Movement and the 1960s,* Book 2, Chapters 1 and 3)

Patricia (Zelkovsky) Salamone

Bob Sanderson

Harriette Schwartz

Iris Shapiro

Randy Sheets

Milton Sirota

Howard Smead (for excerpts from "Ten Years After")

Barry Smith

John Sokirka

Lynn Spencer

Tom Sperry

Debbie Stelnik

John Straub

Stephen Teso

Jackie Watkins

Joanne Wilson-Kelly

Johnny Winter

Donny York (member of Sha Na Na)

Richard Younger

Quotes are credited to the following:

STU FOX INTERVIEWS:

Tom Constanten

Richie Havens

Michael Lang

Country Joe McDonald

Jocko Marcellino

Melanie

Barry Melton

Fito de la Parra

PETER LINDBLAD INTERVIEWS *(GOLDMINE MAGAZINE):*

Mickey Hart

Fito de la Parra

Leslie West

ELLIOT TIBER'S "HOW WOODSTOCK HAPPENED":

Ken Babbs

Bert Feldman

Lou Newman

Al Romm

Joel Rosenman

Mary Sanderson

Wayne Saward

Arnold Skolnick

John Szefc

Art Vassmer

VICTOR KAHN (BERTSOMMER.COM):

Bert Sommer

Artie Kornfeld

Ira Stone

ADDITIONAL PHOTOS:

Barry Smith

James Riley

Joanne Hague

Gerry Bernicky

Sullivan County Democrat
Callicoon, New York
Ted Waddell, photographer

Brad Littleproud

Chipmonck Archives

Associated Press

Heritage Auction Galleries

Thanks to Frame Discreet (Justin Lovell) of Toronto, Ontario, www.framediscreet.com for the restoration and digitizing of rare 8mm Woodstock film footage.

Chapter One

VISIONS OF AQUARIUS

THE CREATION OF THE 1969 WOODSTOCK MUSIC AND ARTS FAIR

"For most of America's youth of the 1960s, the search for personal identity that varied from the traditional values and aspirations of our parents was the priority of the day," recalls Don Aters, famed rock music photographer and historian from New Albany, Indiana.

Don Aters in high school.

"The sixties saw the golden age of rock and roll, the advent of psychedelica, and the turmoil of the most violent times in American history. The migration to Woodstock was a gathering of 'Rainbow Warriors.' We were communal, culturally diverse, and in search of universal peace through the music that defined our generation. With Vietnam raging and shown daily on television as well as the front page of every newspaper, it seemed to us that cultural acceptance was imminent, and that music would be the universal elixir."

Following his discharge from the military, the sights and sounds of the West Coast and the allure of "hippiedom" seemed more viable to Aters than the death and destruction in Southeast Asia. "I was 21 years old, and earlier that year I was indirectly implicated in a civil rights riot in downtown Louisville, Kentucky. I was struck in the face with a heavy pipe, spent 14 days in a coma, and given a poor prognosis for full recovery. A few months later I was on the Pennsylvania Turnpike to join the assumed 25,000 participants expected at the Woodstock Music & Arts Festival. The lengthy sojourn seemed more of an excursion to a tropical rain forest, and when we arrived, the burgeoning crowd was overflowing from Yasgur's farm. We—nearly 500,000 'flower children'—became a beacon in a sea of despair for a world that seemed at odds with everything, including peace and love. During those few days in August of '69, the youth of America brought the world to its knees in a humbling display of confusion as to how a gathering of this magnitude could exist without any of the typical confrontations expected from the 'mainstream.'

Arnold Skolnick's classic Woodstock poster.

The migration to Woodstock was a gathering of 'Rainbow Warriors.' We were communal, culturally diverse, and in search of universal peace through the music that defined our generation.

"Critics of the counterculture, the cultural revolution, the inhabitants of Haight-Ashbury, and those who attended this historical event are also those who adopted the phrase, *'Take nothing but memories, leave nothing but footprints.'* For those of us who experienced those damp and cloudy days long ago, we represent the majority of today's population, and we remain as a community of collective souls who embrace our past and look towards the future."

As in all events, it is the media that holds the power to shape how history is remembered and perceived—making more out of what was less, and, conversely, making less out of what was more. Nowhere is this truer than with Woodstock. In researching *Woodstock, Peace, Music and Memories,* a consistent theme emerged from those who recollected a time in their youth some 40 years ago: pride in the accomplishments of a generation of displaced youth, briefly showing the world how things could be if they were in charge. And a disappointment in how the media, charged with a mission to reduce the event to "reckless sex, drugs, and rock 'n roll," irresponsible hedonism, held Woodstock as proof against a youth culture that was questioning authority and threatening the conservative status quo. A symbol of 1960s excess. Unfortunately, as do many historic victims of the media, Woodstock, too, has maintained its well-spun misperception as something more infamous than significant.

As those once youthful witnessess to this event become the more senior members of our culture, it's time to set the record straight.

"For all those naysayers who know little about what we represented so long ago, we are the Woodstock generation," says Aters. "The memories remain, as do most of us, and so do our ideals. Now 40 years later, a toast to the most sensational event in the annals of contemporary history, a toast to those who orchestrated the Herculean festival, and most of all, 'cheers' to all of us. May we forever be the torchbearers for universal acceptance. Rock in peace!"

Take nothing but memories, leave nothing but footprints
— Chief Seattle

Photo by Cornelius Alexy

Woodstock at its height.

Photo by Derek Redmond and Paul Campbell

A generation brought together.

The Band.

Carlos Santana.

Photos by David Marks (3rd Ear Music/Hidden Years Music Archives 1969-2009)

On a shortlist of historical events, Woodstock has remained part of the cultural lexicon. As Arnold Skolnick, the artist who designed Woodstock's dove-and-guitar symbol, described: "Something was tapped, a nerve, in this country, and everybody just came."

From Aug. 15 -17,1969, the Woodstock Music and Arts Fair held in the Catskill Mountains of New York's Sullivan County, on Max Yasgur's farm in the town of Bethel, was mecca to an A-list of the top performers of rock, folk, and popular music of the time. The rural Borscht Belt area, best known for farming and summer vacationing, would be transformed overnight, briefly becoming New York State's second largest city of more than 450,000 people.

Costing more than $2.4 million, Woodstock was sponsored by four very different and very young men: John Roberts, Joel Rosenman, Artie Kornfeld, and Michael Lang. Twenty-four-year-old John Roberts was heir to a drugstore and toothpaste manufacturing fortune and supplied the money. Roberts' slightly hipper friend, Joel Rosenman, 26, was the son of a prominent Long Island orthodontist and had just graduated from Yale Law School. Roberts and Rosenman met on a golf course in the fall of '66, and by the winter of 1967, they shared an apartment, contemplating their future. Their thought and hope was to create a screwball situation comedy for television, a male version of "I Love Lucy." To get plot ideas for the sitcom, Roberts and Rosenman put a classified ad in the *Wall Street Journal* and the *New York Times* in March 1968: "Young Men with Unlimited Capital looking for interesting, legitimate investment opportunities and business propositions."

Artie Kornfeld, 25, was already well established in the music business. He was Capitol Record's first vice president of rock music, and was the company's connection to the rockers whose music was starting to sell millions of records.

Michael Lang, 24, was described by friends as a cosmic pixie with a head full of curly black hair that bounced to his shoulders and who rarely wore shoes. In 1968, Lang had produced the two-day Miami Pop Festival, which drew 40,000 people. Later that same year, Lang was managing a rock band and wanted to sign a record deal, so he brought his proposal to Kornfeld at Capitol Records in December. Lang knew that he and Artie had both grown up in Bensonhurst, Brooklyn, and used that as his edge, telling the company's receptionist that he was "from the neighborhood."

Woodstock co-creator and promoter Kornfeld remembers: "One day, my secretary buzzed me to say, 'Mike Lang is here to see you.' I asked if he had an appointment and she answered, 'No, he doesn't, but he said to tell you he's from Bensonhurst.' With guys from the neighborhood, you let them in! Michael had all this hair sticking out and I was pretty straight, and to me, he looked like the 'king of the hippies.' He had this terrible band called 'The Train' and he wanted me to get them a development deal with Capitol. To make a long story short, we took them into the studio and the session was a disaster. Whether we were drinking too much red wine or whatever, the only thing that came out of that was the beginnings of our friendship.

"Over time, Michael ended up staying at my place with me and my wife, Linda, and we'd spend nights talking and rambling until morning. One night, we were playing bumper pool, smoking some great Columbian, and Michael started teasing that I didn't go to clubs anymore to see live acts; truth being, after 12 years in the music business I'd become too busy. That's when I said, 'Michael, I have a great idea. What if we had all the money in the world—we could rent a Broadway theater, have a concert, and just invite our friends. We could get Jimi Hendrix, The Rolling Stones, Creedence Clearwater, Sly Stone, The Beatles, and every other act that we would love to see perform. We won't charge anything, and it will be one of the greatest parties of all time.' I thought I'd finally get to see all these acts, and Michael thought we should host our festival in Woodstock, New York. Michael also dreamt of a recording studio in Woodstock. It was a popular artist's colony. People like Paul Butterfield, Bob Dylan, The Band, and Richie Havens were also living there, and it had really become the 'in' place. We talked endlessly about putting on this show and hoped that maybe 100,000 people would show up, or at least 50,000. My wife, Linda, thought maybe half a million because those love-ins were getting 10,000 people, and if we had all those acts.... I would say we dreamt about this for months and figured it would stay just that—a dream."

Kornfeld continues: "One day Michael's lawyer called to tell us that there were two guys [John Robert and Joel Rosenman] advertising in the *New York Times,* who had unlimited capitol for investment, and he convinced me to get in touch with them. We pitched the idea for the recording studio in Woodstock, and John and Joel saw the opportunity to finance it through our idea of a music festival. We got backing for our dream, and the deal was sealed."

Poster by David Byrd

The four met in February 1969, and by the end of their third meeting, the little party had snowballed into a bucolic concert for 50,000, the world's largest rock and roll show ever, and the four partners formed Woodstock Ventures Inc., named after the hip little Ulster County town.

The team found a site owned by Howard Mills Jr., and for $10,000, Woodstock Ventures leased a tract of land in the town of Wallkill.

"We drove up to Wallkill and saw the property," Rosenman says. "We talked to Howard Mills and made a deal. The vibes weren't right there. It was an industrial park," but Roberts insisted that they needed a site immediately. The 300-acre Mills Industrial Park offered perfect access. It was less than a mile from Route 17, which linked to major thoroughfares, and it had the needed essentials like electricity and water lines. In late March or early April, Rosenman told Wallkill officials the concert would feature jazz bands and folk singers. He also said that 50,000 people would attend, if they were lucky.

In the cultural-political atmosphere of 1969, promoters Kornfeld and Lang knew it was important to pitch Woodstock in a way that would appeal to their peers' sense of independence. Lang wanted to call the festival an "Aquarian Exposition," capitalizing on the zodiacal reference from the musical "Hair," and he had an ornate poster designed featuring the Water Bearer. By early April, the promoters were carefully cultivating the Woodstock image in the underground press, in publications such as the *Village Voice* and *Rolling Stone* magazine. Ads began to run in the *New York Times* and the Middleton, New York *Times Herald-Record* in May. For Kornfeld, Woodstock wasn't a matter of building stages, signing acts or even selling tickets; for him, the festival was a state of mind, a happening that would exemplify the generation. The event's publicity shrewdly appropriated the counterculture's symbols and catch phrases. "The cool PR image was intentional," he said.

Advertising coupon for Woodstock.

The group settled on the concrete slogan of "Three Days of Peace and Music" and downplayed the highly conceptual theme of Aquarius. The promoters figured *peace* would link the antiwar sentiment to the rock concert, and also wanting to avoid any violence, they thought a slogan with *peace* in it would help keep order.

The Woodstock dove is really a catbird. "I was staying on Shelter Island off Long Island, and I was drawing catbirds all the time," said artist Arnold Skolnick. "As soon as Ira Arnold [a copywriter on the project] called with the copy-approved 'Three Days of Peace and Music,' I just took the razor blade and cut that catbird out of the sketchpad I was using. First, it sat on a flute. I was listening to jazz at the time, and I guess that's why. But anyway, it sat on a flute for a day, and I finally ended up putting it on a guitar."

Kornfeld adds, "With John and Joel's initial investment, I had a small budget for advertising, and I couldn't imagine that it was just hippies in the Village in New York City who had no money, who would be into this. They wouldn't be able to come up with $8 for a ticket for each day of the festival. I took an ad out in the *New York Times*, the *Village Other*, and the *Village Voice* with a coupon that they had to fill out for more information. When those coupons started coming in, I thought, 'Wow, 89 percent of these kids are white, middle-class, college types.' With the money I had left, I went to the radio stations, and with my promotion skills, advertised directly to reach those kids. I researched, so I knew when they would be on the beach or in their car listening, and I used airplanes to pull banners advertising the event. That ad, which first ran on my wedding anniversary, ended up bringing in a million and half dollars to get this thing up and running."

Woodstock Ventures was aiming to book the biggest rock and roll bands in America, but the rockers were reluctant to sign with an untested outfit that might be unable to deliver.

"To get the contracts, we had to have the credibility, and to get the credibility, we had to have the contracts," Rosenman says. Woodstock Ventures solved the problem by promising paychecks unheard of in 1969. The big breakthrough came with the signing of the top psychedelic band of the day, Jefferson Airplane, for the incredible sum of $12,000, double their usual pay for gigs. Creedence Clearwater Revival signed for $11,500. The Who then came in for $12,500, and the rest of the acts started to fall in line. "We paid Jimi Hendrix $32,000. He was the headliner, and that's what he wanted," Rosenman says.

The residents of Wallkill had heard of hippies, drugs, and rock concerts, but after the Woodstock advertising hit the major newspapers and radio stations, local residents knew that a three-day rock show [maybe the biggest ever] was coming. Woodstock Ventures' employees looked like hippies, and in the minds of many people, long hair and shabby clothes were associated with left-wing politics and drug use. The new ideas about reordering society were threatening to many people, and the Wallkill Zoning Board of Appeals officially banned Woodstock on July 15, 1969, to the applause of residents. Two weeks earlier, the town board had passed a law requiring a permit for any gatherings greater than 5,000 people.

PREMIER TALENT ASSOCIATES, INC. / 200 WEST 57TH STREET New York, N.Y. 10019 • 757-4300

JUL 30 1969

AGREEMENT made this 27th day of JUNE, 1969, between NEW ACTION LTD. FURNISHING THE SERVICES OF THE WHO (hereinafter referred to as "ARTIST") and WOODSTOCK VENTURES INC. (hereinafter referred to as "PURCHASER").

THIS CONTRACT IS ONLY VALID SUBJECT TO IMMIGRATION AND NATURALIZATION CLEARANCE.

It is mutually agreed between the parties as follows:

The PURCHASER hereby engages the ARTIST and the ARTIST hereby agrees to perform the engagement hereinafter provided, upon all of the terms and conditions herein set forth, including those hereof entitled "Additional Terms and Conditions."

1. PLACE OF ENGAGEMENT AQUARIAN FESTIVAL GROUNDS
   Exact address WALLKILL, NEW YORK
2. DATE(s) OF ENGAGEMENT AUGUST ~~17~~ 16, 1969
3. HOURS OF ENGAGEMENT ONE (1) ONE (1) HOUR SHOW. PLEASE ADVISE SHOW TIMES.
4. REHEARSAL(s) REPORT TIME 12 NOON.
5. FULL PRICE AGREED UPON: TWELVE THOUSAND FIVE HUNDRED DOLLARS FLAT ($12,500.00)

All payments shall be paid by certified check, money order, bank draft or cash as follows:

(a) $ 6,250.00 shall be paid by PURCHASER to and in the name of ARTIST'S agent, PREMIER TALENT ASSOCIATES, INC., not later than IMMEDIATELY;

(b) $ 6,250.00 shall be paid by PURCHASER to ARTIST not later than IN CASH ONLY PRIOR TO SHOW DAY OF ENGAGEMENT.;

(c) Additional payments, if any, shall be paid by PURCHASER to ARTIST not later than

PURCHASER shall first apply any and all receipts derived from the engagement herein to the payments required hereunder: All payments shall be made in full without any deductions whatsoever.

RECEIVED 7/15 6250 rr

6. SCALE OF ADMISSION

****ARTIST IS TO RECEIVE 100% STAR BILLING. ARTISTS ARE BILLED IN ALPHABETICAL ORDER. THIS IS A FESTIVAL CONCEPT; THEREFORE PLACEMENT OF ACT IS AT THE DISCRETION OF PROMOTER.
FB:rr

Return all signed copies to agent:
Premier Talent Associates, Inc.

NEW ACTION LTD. FURNISHING THE SERVICES OF THE WHO
By [signature]

WOODSTOCK VENTURES INC. (PURCHASER)
SIGN HERE By [signature: Michael Lang]
Address: 513 A 6th AVENUE
N. Y. C.
Phone: (212) CH3-6260

THE ABOVE SIGNATURES CONFIRM THAT THE PARTIES HAVE READ AND APPROVE EACH AND ALL OF THE "ADDITIONAL TERMS AND CONDITIONS" SET FORTH ON THE REVERSE SIDE HEREOF.
PLEASE INITIAL BACK OF CONTRACT.

Photo courtesy Brad Littleproud

Contract for The Who to play at Woodstock.

"The law they passed excluded one thing and one thing only—Woodstock," says Al Romm, then-editor of the *Times Herald-Record,* which editorialized against the law.

Paul Novak was growing up in Wallkill and lived about half a mile from what was to be the festival site. "I was only 14 at the time," remembers Paul. "I was a budding guitar player and totally fascinated with the unfolding events... locals vs. hippies. I remember wandering up to the Wallkill site that summer, and even sneaking into the barn that the organizers were using as an office. From the outside, you could see hippies building a stage, but the inside of that barn was a beehive

Photo by John De Lorenzo

Long hair was referred to as the "freak flag" waved by hippies.

THE TIMES HERALD · RECORD Thursday, July 24, 1969 5

Rock fete readies Bethel site; few protest

By CHARLIE CRIST

WHITE LAKE

Supervisor Daniel J Amatucci reported Wednesday getting about 20 phone calls opposing the Woodstock Ventures' Aquarian Festival in the town

"The opposition," he said "seemed to be from a few individuals and was not organized He said there had been no threats of "legal entanglements "

Meanwhile members of the festival troupe worked on preparations at the Max Yasgur farm site despite the rain. Spokesmen for the group said everything would be ready when the festival opens Aug 15

Frederick W. V. Schadt, Bethel Town Attorney, asked why a public hearing had not been held, said he could think of no reason for one.

There is nothing in the Bethel town law that I could find that requires a public hearing " he said

Schadt said the town board, while approving the festival could not disapprove" since no ordinance was violated

Publicity personnel reported Wednesday that 20 000 sales are expected in the Orange-Sullivan-Ulster county area with most of the audience coming from across the nation

Mel Lawrence operations director said two weeks are needed to complete the stage but said the company is not alarmed over the late start owing to switching location from the Town of Wallkill near Middletown to Sullivan County

Seventy five workers are on the scene, some of them putting in 20 hours a day.

Among the workers are college and high school professors and art students

Chris Langhardt of New York University for instance, will be in charge of stage production He is in a similar capacity at NYU

James Mitchell the Woodstock purchasing agent, a teacher-director of theater at NYU will mastermind this part of the production

John Morris "director of productions is a former operator of Filmore East in New York He and a partner are investing in a multi-million dollar hotel construction project in St Thomas W I

Uchip Monck, the production supervisor, is staging the lighting facilities and is considered by stage people one of the outstanding theater lighting experts in the country.

Members of the work crews slogged through mud and high grass most of them wet to the knees from the week s rains and getting wetter as the rains continued

The kids "don't mind this " said Rona Elliott a public relations staffer " This is part of their thing the same as the guy who goes hunting or fishing in the rain

As the festival workers pressed to organize the site others began an area canvass and community relations program Led by the Rev Donald Ganoung, the festival representatives will talk with area residents.

Comparing our reception here to that of the Town of Wallkill we are overwhelmed " said Miss Elliott

Jay Drevers looks over transit surveying Yasgur Farm, latest site of Aquarian Festival in Town of Bethel, Sullivan County as Steve Ostrom and Jerry Gerth handle other surveying chores Festival moved this week to the Sullivan County location -- TH-Record photo by Charlie Crist

of activity filled with desks and telephones ringing. All those long-haired folks were so out of place in our little hick town. That stage was already half constructed when Wallkill wanted out. There were already so many people coming, and this scared a lot of folks. All the work that had been completed to that point was abandoned, and the structure sat for years—an unfinished monument to what might have been."

Elliot Tiber read about Woodstock getting tossed out of Wallkill. He owned the El Monaco, a White Lake resort of 80 rooms with nearly all of them empty, and keeping it going was draining his savings. But for all of Tiber's troubles, he had one thing that was very valuable to Woodstock Ventures: a Bethel town permit to run a music festival.

"I think it cost $12 or $8 or something like that," Tiber said. "It was very vague. It just said that I had permission to run an arts and music festival. That's it." The permit was actually for the White Lake Music and Arts Festival, a very small event that Tiber had dreamed up to increase business at the hotel. Tiber called Woodstock Ventures, not even knowing whom to ask for. Lang got the message and went out to Elliot's place the next day [probably July 18] to take a look around. Tiber's festival site was 15 swampy acres behind the resort.

"Michael looked at that and said, 'This isn't big enough,'" Tiber recalls. "So I said, 'Why don't we go see my friend Max Yasgur? He's been selling me milk and cheese for years. He's got a big farm out there in Bethel.'"

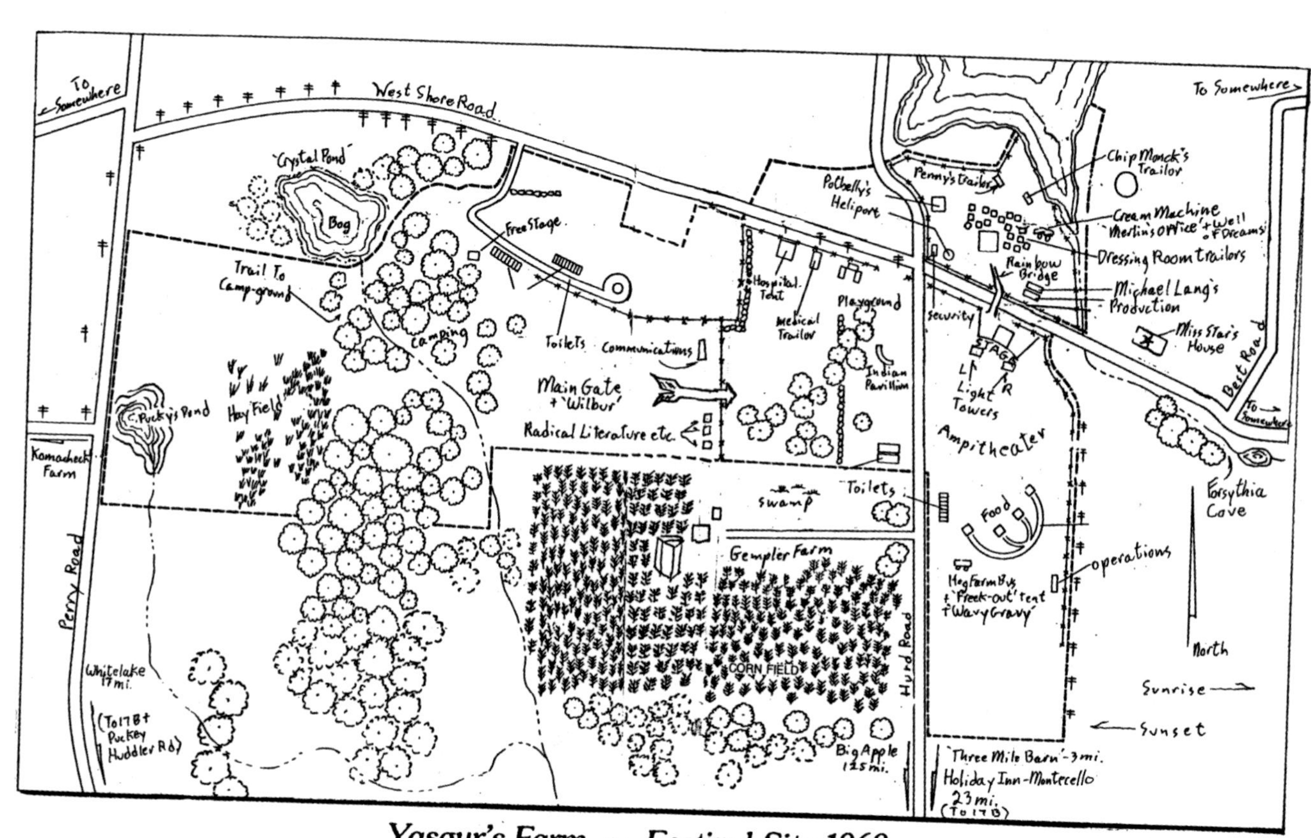

Original festival site design for Woodstock.

Map courtesy Woodstock Ventures LLC.

"It was magic," Lang said. It was perfect—the sloping bowl, a little rise for the stage, a lake in the background.

Something was tapped, a nerve, in this country, and everybody just came.

Promoters claim they can handle 150,000

WHITE LAKE

Can up to 150,000 folk-rock music fans be accommodated in an open Sullivan County pasture during three days in August?

Woodstock Ventures, backers of the massive Aquarian Exposition now planned for the Town of Bethel, said Monday that they can and will be

That assurance plus supporting promises are essentially the same ones that didn't cut much ice in the Orange County Town of Wallkill. There, the festival has been banned by the town's zoning board of appeals and, to boot, faces widespread opposition by Town of Wallkill citizenry.

Miss Pat Costello, a Woodstock spokesman in New York, said Monday that plans include a security detail of 300 hand-picked police officers, a corps of production men, and a nationally-known food concessionaire

The festival, she said, will be an around-the-clock entertainment extravaganza for the anticipated 150,000 persons attending

Miss Costello described the 3-day event as a virtual camp-in aimed toward the younger set who bring their own trailers, tents, and sleeping facilities

Cost of the production is estimated in excess of $1 million with contracts already signed with many of the national and international stars

The list includes Jimi Hendrix, The Band, Blood Sweat and Tears, Jeff Beck Group, Crosby, Stills and Nash, Johnny Winter, Iron Butterfly, Jefferson Airplane, Janis Joplin, Grateful Dead, Credence Clearwater Revival, Canned Heat, Ravi Shankar, The Incredible String Band, Richie Havens, Arlo Guthrie, Tim Hardin, Joan Baez, Sweetwater Mountain, Joe Cocker, Ten Years Later, and Keef Hartley.

Miss Costello said there would be movies, song festivals, poetry sessions, films and other kinds of entertainment going on around the clock

The main Friday show will start at 4 p m , ending in the early morning hours, while Saturday and Sunday the shows start at 1 p m and end at 2 a m.

The stage is to be built on a revolving circular base

There will be no shelter or seating facilities for the audience, she said Festival goers would supply their own chairs or sit on the grass.

As to sanitary facilities, Miss Costello said that the company was prepared to have portable units far in excess of the need. Water would probably be trucked in tank trucks, she said.

The security detail would be under the direction of Wesley Pomeroy, a former associate administrator of law enforcement in the U S Justice Dept

He was also a special assistant to the U S attorney general, undersheriff in San Mateo, Calif , and in charge of security at the 1964 Republican Convention in San Francisco

The security men will be unarmed and will not carry night sticks, she said

Miss Costello said that parking areas will be far enough away from the main festival that 100 shuttle buses will have to be used to the site

The food concession is to be handled by Nathans of Coney Island, she said, adding that, besides the normal foods there will be special health and micro-biotic foods

Tickets are $7 per show, $18 for three days and $13 for two days

The Woodstock company is building a recording studio at Woodstock in Ulster County and hopes to have proceeds from the festival to further develop the studio she said

President of the firm is John Roberts, a Graduate of the University of Pennsylvania and Annenberg School of Communications One of his four vice presidents is Joel Rosenman, a Princeton and Yale Graduate and a member of the New York Bar Association

Michael Lang is listed as executive producer and, according to the New York office, has produced other festivals including one in Miami, Fla.

Miss Costello, who said she had been at the Newport, R I rock festival where there was considerable disruption, said this festival will be equipped "far better than Newport "

"One of the problems," she said of Newport, "was the fact that 22,000 persons were inside a festival area and 27,000 were outside with no facilities "

"This will not happen here," she said

--CHARLIE CRIST

Photo by Cornelius Alexy

This truck, loaded with psychedelic equipment for the Aquarian Festival in Bethel, flipped over as it turned into Rt. 17B near Monticello Raceway Wednesday night. The driver, 20-year-old Stuart M. Hutter of Flushing, Queens, was unhurt and no summonses were issued. --TH-Record photo by Gil Weisinger

Trooper A. J. Raab, Jr., on special assignment in Sullivan County, mans a temporary police telephone and communications system in the Iroquois Hunting Club main clubhouse, six miles from the festival site. --TH-Record photo by Charlie Crist

Text by Denis Thoet

City of 150,000 - for 3 days

WHITE LAKE

While mankind is still scratching his collective head about the significance of last month's moon shot Sullivan County residents will soon have to ponder the meaning of the Aquarian Exposition.

Rising out of its own magnificent desolation of 19th century farmland in the Town of Bethel is a city of the most freaked-out, turned-on and perhaps the happiest youths in this country, drawn here by the giant sounds of the biggest names in the electronic rock world. Hendrix, Janis Joplin, Donovan, Canned Heat, Blood, Sweat and Tears, and more, man.

For three days the population of this new city -- 150,000 -- will outnumber by three to one the present whole population of the county. Then it will disappear with few traces left a month from now -- except for the $3-4 million exposition officials estimate will be dumped during the affair.

The center of this city of light and sound is a launching pad-like stage flanked by giant yellow scaffolding towers to hold the amplifier and lighting systems. Thursday night, not everything was ready for the 4 p.m. blastoff today, but Aquarian officials maintain it will be.

Two thousand workers hired by Woodstock Ventures, Inc. of New York were to work through the night and until the four o'clock countdown. Most of the pavilions housing press, entertainers, and concessions were only half completed Thursday night.

"Everybody's here," said one girl with a laugh. "People I lived with in California and others I know from Massachusetts are here. When I see them on the road, we just go 'wow!' "

They came in their jeans and leather vests, headbands and jeweled pendants -- boys without shirts, girls without bras -- from all over the country.

They came in a stream that began as a trickle at the beginning of the week. Now Rt. 17B, the only access road, is bumper-to-bumper for ten miles on each side of the Hurd Road entrance despite the best efforts of state police to direct and move traffic.

They came and camped in two big hay fields -- 25,000 had pitched their tents by noon Thursday. But most of the new arrivals simply found places to park their sleeping bags and stayed there, lining Hurd Road and West Shore Road and eating slush balls.

At Leon's Lake behind the festival site choice camping spots have been heavily packed with people and swimmers -- many wearing no clothes at all -- cooling their heels and their heads in the water.

Campers spilled over into a small bungalow colony owned by Ben Leon, who, at a fairly spry 81, drove them out periodically during the week.

"The sheriff promised me protection and I don't have it," he said excitedly. "Last night I was awake most of the night with these kids coming by and stopping here. They were making so much noise I had to come out with my 30.06 and I shot it ten times into the air. That got them moving. Ten, fifteen years ago, I could lick the whole bunch of them."

Perhaps the home closest to the sights and sounds of the new city belongs to Jesse and Edna Starr on West Shore Road.

Both in their 70s, they sit at the front window and watch the streams of people and cars on the road.

A tent city has sprung up overnight in the background of the festival's 60- by 40-foot stage. Thousands of hippie campers have swarmed over the 600 acres of the Max Yasgur farm in the Town of Bethel. --TH-Record photo by Charlie Crist

Yasgur met Lang in the alfalfa field. This time, Lang liked the lay of the land. "It was magic," Lang said. It was perfect—the sloping bowl, a little rise for the stage, a lake in the background, and the deal was sealed right there on the spot.

Lang recalls, "Max and I were walking on the rise above the bowl. When we started to talk business, he was figuring how much he was going to lose in his crop and how much it was going to cost him to reseed the field. He was a sharp guy, ol' Max, and he was figuring everything up with a pencil and paper, wetting the pencil tip with his tongue. I remember shaking his hand, and that's the first time I noticed that he had only three fingers, but his grip was like iron. He'd cleared that land himself."

Within days after meeting Yasgur, Lang brought the rest of the Ventures crew up, but by then, Yasgur was wise to Woodstock and the price had gone up considerably. Woodstock Ventures kept the negotiations secret, lest it repeat what had happened in Wallkill. The Woodstock partners have since admitted that they were engaged in "creative deception." They told Bethel officials that they were expecting 50,000 people, tops, when all along they knew that Woodstock would draw far more.

"I was pretty manipulative," Lang admits. "The figure at Wallkill was 50,000, and we just stuck with it. I was planning on a quarter-million people, but we didn't want to scare anyone."

Reprinted with permission from the Times Herald-Record.

With Yasgur's assistance, the appropriate permits were obtained, but as news of the festival spread, it stimulated local opposition. An anonymous party erected a 2-1/2 -by-4-foot sign that read, "Local People Speak Out/Stop Max's Music Festival/No 150,000 Hippies Here/Buy No Milk." The Yasgurs had been having second thoughts about their decision to lease their land, but after they saw that sign, they were determined to go through with it.

As July became August, Vassmer's General Store in Kauneonga Lake was doing a great business in kegs of nails and cold cuts. The buyers were long-haired construction guys who were carving Yasgur's pasture into an amphitheater.

"They told me, 'Mr. Vassmer, you ain't seen nothing yet,' and by golly, they were right," remembers Art Vassmer, owner of the store. Abe Wagner knew that little Bethel, with a population of 3,900, wasn't set to handle the coming flood of humanity. Two weeks before the festival, Woodstock Ventures had already sold 180,000 tickets, and a week before the festival, Yasgur's farm didn't look much like a concert site. "It was like they were building a house, except there was a helicopter pad," Vassmer says.

Photo courtesy Brad Littleproud

Vassmer's General Store, Kauneonga Lake (Bethel), New York.

A Festival Site Rises from Max Yasgur's Farm

Photo by David Marks (3rd Ear Music/Hidden Years Music Archives 1969-2009)

An early Woodstock arrival looks toward the concession area in a pristine field.

Photo by Cornelius Alexy

Performers pavilion being built behind newly installed fencing.

Photo by Cornelius Alexy

It took immense amounts of lumber and plywood to build the Woodstock stage.

Photo by Cornelius Alexy

Photo by Cornelius Alexy

Building the stage.

Photo by Cornelius Alexy

Massive cranes lift materials and raise sound towers. The stage was accidentally built around the cranes, making them impossible to remove.

Photo by Cornelius Alexy

Four scaffold towers are raised to hold the speaker system and lighting.

Photo by Chris Langhart

The performers pavilion was a log pole and tarpaulin design to complement the rural setting.

Photo by Chris Langhart

Thousands of tents, trailers and cars would take over the field behind the pavilion as one of many "unofficial" campgrounds.

Photo by Chris Langhart

The Indian pavilion was to showcase the arts and heritage of the East. As with the "Arts Fair" component of the festival, it did not materialize.

Photo by Chris Langhart

Chris Langhart submitted a design for the stage roof. It was rejected for the truss and sail design.

Photo by Cornelius Alexy

A view of West Shore Road that ran behind the stage. A wooden bridge was constructed across the road joining the stage to the back stage performers area.

As Aquarius rose in Bethel, Artie Kornfeld had bigger fish to fry. "What was paramount to the success of the festival was the need to ensure that the festival would be peaceful," Kornfeld says. "At that time of unrest in America, I knew that I had to go meet with the Black Panthers, the SDS, and Abbie Hoffman, and become friends to divert any possible trouble prior to the concert. It took time, but I was able to get guarantees that 'Three Days of Peace and Music' would be just that."

Staff pass. Photo by David Marks (3rd Ear Music/ Hidden Years Music Archives 1969-2009)

© Lisa Law

Lisa and Pilar Law.

Harriette Schwartz, 19, was born and raised in the Bronx, New York, and landed a great job after high school with Warner Bros./Seven Arts in the city. Because of this position, she learned of the plans for Woodstock. Michael Wadleigh, the filmmaker for the Woodstock documentary, and his crew had been given offices there in the Tisch Building at 666 Fifth Avenue.

"They were a bit different, sitting on their desks with their feet up on their chairs, but always pleasant enough," Schwartz remembers. As often is the case in the workplace, everyone knew why they were there, and when a good-looking guy from the mailroom named Alan asked her to go to Woodstock, she said yes. Alan was from Sheepshead Bay in Brooklyn, and they drove up to Bethel the weekend before to check things out.

"Little did I know the prequel I was witnessing," Schwartz says. "It was a huge, open, grassy cow pasture onto which these huge metal stanchions were being erected. It was a hilly, tranquil, and placid venue. The day was sunny, the sky was blue, and you never would have guessed that such a peaceful setting would become home to half a million celebrants dancing in the rain and mud, just one week later."

Lisa Law, 24, of Santa Fe, New Mexico, remembers that at the 1969 Aspen Meadows Summer Solstice in New Mexico, Stan Goldstein [campground supervisor for Woodstock] asked the Hog Farm and the Jook Savages to handle the coordination of the campgrounds at the festival.

"Since we were a large communal group," Law says, "he thought we would know how to take care of masses of people, especially if they were taking drugs, as we were well-versed on the subject. We agreed. Our party of about 85, with 15 Indians from the Santa Fe Indian School, turned up on the assigned day at the Albuquerque Airport to take the jumbo jet the organizers sent to fly us to the festival. [My husband] Tom and I decided to take our tepee. The handlers at the airport looked like Keystone Kops loading the poles into the baggage compartment. That had to be a first."

Jean Nichols, 24, was returning to the United States from Vancouver, Canada, after the birth of her daughter. On the way, they stopped at Merry Prankster leader Ken Kesey's farm, and from there she met up with the Hog Farm. Jean remembers, "We were told that we'd be setting up a place where the people would be camping, the free stage, plus we'd have our own space."

Thirty-three-year-old Hugh Romney [later taking the name Wavy Gravy, given to him by B. B. King], first among the commune's equals, donned a Smokey-the-Bear suit and armed himself with a bottle of seltzer and a rubber shovel. When they stepped off the plane at Kennedy Airport on Monday, Aug. 11, the Hog Farmers were met by the World Press, who informed them they had also been assigned the task of doing security.

"My god, they made us the cops," Wavy said. "'Well, do you feel secure?' I asked. The guy answered, 'Yeah,' so I said, 'See, it's working already.' That's when he asked what we were going to use for crowd control. I told him 'cream pies and seltzer water.'" He and the members of the New Mexico commune constituted themselves as the "Please Force."

Lisa Law remembers, "We got a flash that the concert was going to be a monster and we had better prepare for the onslaught if we were to take care of the masses of hungry souls who wouldn't have enough food with them, or enough money to buy any, so somebody had to go into the city for supplies."

Fellow Hog Farmer Peter Whiterabbit volunteered to be Law's assistant, truck driver, and guide in New York City, where she'd been only once before. With $3,000 from the organizers, she purchased 1,200 pounds of bulgur wheat and rolled oats, two dozen 25-pound boxes of currants, almonds, and dried apricots, 200 pounds of wheat germ, five wooden kegs of soy sauce, and five big kegs of honey. She then bought five huge stainless steel bowls and 35 plastic garbage pails.

Photo by Jean Nichols

Compound for the Earth Light Theatre, who entertained the crowds at the free stage.

Hugh Romney, also known as Wavy Gravy, and the Hog Farm arriving at JFK.

"I figured we would feed some 150,000 people, so I bought 130,000 paper plates, spoons and forks and about 50,000 paper cups. While roaming around Chinatown, I bought a jade Buddha for good luck and to keep the kitchen crew blessed.

"While we were in the city, the crew on site was building the kitchen and the food booths. I had come up with a design for the serving booths, where two people could serve from either side, creating 10 lines for five booths," Law remembers. "We got the kitchen functioning and everything cooking, and out of nowhere came 10 to 15 volunteers at a time, cutting and cooking and serving and having a great time doing it."

About 2 a.m. Tuesday morning, Elliott Tiber recalls, "I didn't sleep well. I woke up and I heard horns and guitars. I look out, and there are five lanes of headlights all the way back. They'd started coming already."

Television actress Bonnie Jean Romney (nee Bonnie Beecher, later taking the name Jahanara) was 27 and married to Wavy. She was in charge of the kitchen and oversaw the crews.

Jahanara Romney in 1969.

Tickets for the contracted "Food for Love" concession stands.

About 2 a.m. Tuesday morning, Elliott Tiber recalls, "I didn't sleep well. I woke up and I heard horns and guitars. I look out, and there are five lanes of headlights all the way back. They'd started coming already."

"Somehow I had access to this little scooter-type thing," Jahanara remembers. "It was like a motorcycle with a wheelbarrow on the back. Yasgur's dairy farm was just up on 17B, and they had a place where you could buy their products, so we made arrangements with them to get fresh yogurt, which I was able to get and bring back using this little vehicle. There were so many people already there that we started to serve on Tuesday."

Eight miles away, *Times Herald-Record* harness racing reporter John Szefc was working on a feature story at the Monticello Raceway when he caught a glimpse of Route 17B. "It was 11 a.m., more than 24 hours before the concert, and traffic was already backed up all the way down Route 17B to Route 17, a distance of 10 miles. That's when I knew this was going to be big. Really significant," he says.

For Randy Sheets, 19, from Long Island, New York, it was the summer after his first year of college. "Late at night, my friend Chris and I would often lie on the rug in my parent's living room,

This original "welcome sign" can still be found in Bethel, New York today. Courtesy of Larry Houman. In memory of Carol Hector Houman. (Owned by Jerry and Kay Hector)

Photo by Joanne Hague

in front of a fan, and listen to WNEW FM, the New York City-based progressive rock station. My parents had long since gone to bed, and we would listen to the late night deejays, Rosco and Allison Steele, 'The Night Bird,' and their sultry, silken voices would somehow help cool the hot summer nights. That was where we started hearing talk of an August festival planned in upstate New York, called Woodstock. My younger brother, Scott, had already bought tickets (he still has them), and the week before the festival, the deejays were talking about the large crowds that were expected. No one had a car of their own, so we prevailed upon our parents to loan us the Ford Country Squire station wagon, and all was a go! We decided to head up early and try and avoid the crowds, so we set out on the Wednesday before.

"Seven of us crammed in the car along with our camping gear—tent, sleeping bags, flashlights, Coleman stove, etc. —and some Goobers, a combination of peanut butter and grape jelly swirled together in a jar," Sheets says. "In the car were my brother Scott, who was a year younger than me, his two friends, Bub and Curtis, my two friends, Chris and Peter, and the younger brother of one of Scott's friends, Jimmy. Before we left, my father handed me his hand-winding 8mm movie camera and a few spools of film. He said he wouldn't be needing it, so I might as well take it along.

"I don't remember much about the drive up even though I was the one driving!" says Randy. "We knew where we were going, and as we got closer we saw hand-printed signs pointing the way. It wasn't too difficult. All you had to do was follow the line. The traffic got heavier as we approached, and we drove until we saw some other folks parked on farmland up to the right. It was slow going for those last few miles with a steady stream of cars all bumper to bumper, and many people walking along both sides of the road. Some folks jumped on the front fenders of our car and got a lift and since we were only creeping along, this was easily accomplished. Food, weed, and drink were being shared among the walkers and the people in cars, and there was a real sense of being a part of something big."

Heading off to History

Still photo taken from 8mm film, courtesy Randy Sheets.

Randy Sheets and friends getting closer to Woodstock.

Still photo taken from 8mm film, courtesy Randy Sheets.

Randy Sheets parents' station wagon.

Still photo taken from 8mm film, courtesy Randy Sheets.

Randy's view getting closer to the festival.

We quickly got used to jumping on to 'hitch' a ride, and everyone was just grooving on one another.

Still photo taken from 8mm film, courtesy Randy Sheets.

It was easier said than done.

Still photo taken from 8mm film, courtesy Randy Sheets.

Jimmy Acunto, 15.

Still photo taken from 8mm film, courtesy Randy Sheets.

Randy Sheets, 19.

"When I was 16," recalls Greg Henry of Kearney, New Jersey, "I attended the Atlantic City Pop Fest in early August, where I met a lot of people talking about Woodstock, but I wasn't sure if I could go. The reactions from my parents were mixed. Mom was excited and Dad just shook his head, but I got the ok and went with Bob Wall, my best friend. Neither of us had a car, so we used our thumbs and left early Wednesday morning."

While so many others had to deal with traffic, Greg and Bob had their own set of problems to contend with. "We were stopped by a State Trooper on the New York Thruway, who didn't seem to like us much or the fact that we were going to Woodstock. He made us empty our backpacks, which held a bunch of oranges, cheese, and a butter knife. I guess he wanted to be really thorough in his search and make sure we didn't have anything illegal stuck in those oranges…so he proceeded to stomp on every one. He confiscated our butter knife, told us to be careful, and sent us on our way. Soon after, we were picked up by an army green car with insignias on the doors, and driving was a black gentleman wearing an Army uniform. Right off we thought it was pretty weird, but the ride was very welcome. I noticed a bandage on his wrist, and I could see blood seeping through. He was driving very fast and erratic and kept asking if we wanted to see his gun. Needless to say, we were very nervous by this point, but luckily we started to see a lot of people much like ourselves. We asked the guy to drop us off, but he continued on a few more miles. When he finally stopped the car, he was still insisting that he show us his gun and to our shock, he did, but it wasn't what we were expecting. He opened his pants and exposed himself. 'See my gun' and with that…we were off and running."

On approaching the "official" camping area, Randy Sheets and his friends remember seeing a relatively clear spot off in the fields. "We left the road, drove across the grass and parked among a dozen other cars and tents. We brought a tent, which we soon found leaked badly! Somehow it got set up, and we

Still photo taken from 8mm film, courtesy Randy Sheets.

Randy Sheets' friend, Jimmy.

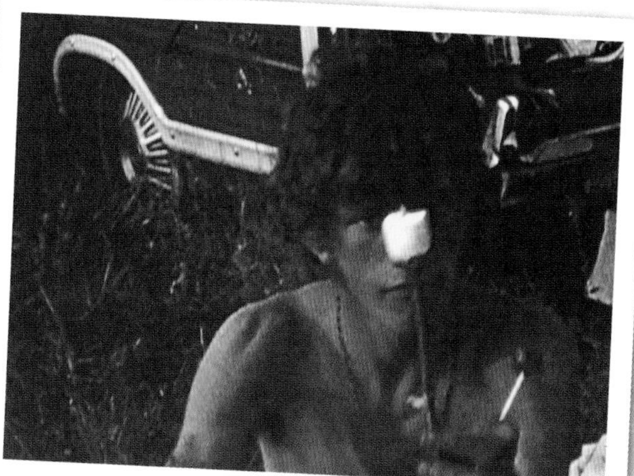

Still photo taken from 8mm film, courtesy Randy Sheets.

Scott Sheets, 17, Randy's brother.

Still photo taken from 8mm film, courtesy Randy Sheets.

Paul "Bub" Smith, 17.

tossed in our gear, headed for the road, and began our march to the festival site. We quickly got used to jumping on car fenders to 'hitch' a ride, and everyone was just grooving on one another. There was this overwhelming feeling of togetherness. We arrived at the site and joined a large crowd that was headed towards a fence that had been rather haphazardly set up. We pushed the fence down very easily, and we headed toward the stage area. It really wasn't a 'pushing down' as much as it was a 'walking down.' There was no malice; it was just meant to be down. We staked out our area, stage left about 10 rows back. They were really good 'seats' and we always made sure we had someone stay back to save them the entire time. We brought a couple of blankets to mark our spot and sit on, and at this point, we were all in a beautiful green meadow of knee high grass. When we found out that the music would last far into the night and early morning, we lugged all our sleeping bags over from the campsite."

Christmas lights were strung in the trees. Sawdust was strewn along the paths. Over the hill, carpenters were still banging nails into the main stage. The Merry Pranksters and the Hog Farmers had built their own alternative stage for anyone who wanted to jam, and the sound system was a space amplifier borrowed from the Grateful Dead.

"We heard music coming from an area to the side of the main stage," says Sheets, "and we wandered down to see what was up. There we found three or four psychedelic buses and a low stage with people sitting around grooving on the music. It seems we happened upon the Hog Farm and the Merry Pranksters' bus, 'Further.'"

Dennis Himes, a 15-year-old from Ridgefield, Connecticut, went to Woodstock with his 17-year-old brother, Geoff, and his friend, Pete. Dennis remembers, "On Thursday night there was a concert on the free stage. I remember somebody making soap bubbles, and when a bubble would float up above the crowd, people would shine their flashlights on it, causing two bright dots of light on the bubble. With several flashlights on all the bubbles, it was a floating constellation of stars."

Still photo taken from 8mm film, courtesy Randy Sheets.

"We found a place to park," said Randy Sheets.

Photo by Cornelius Alexy

The crowd gathers in the concert bowl.

Still photo taken from 8mm film, courtesy Randy Sheets.

Fields became parking lots.

Still photo taken from 8mm film, courtesy Randy Sheets.

Christmas lights were on the fences and in the trees.

Massive speakers perched on tall towers were being set up.

Still photo taken from 8mm film, courtesy Randy Sheets.

Psychedelic buses surrounded the free stage at the Hog Farm encampment.

Still photo taken from 8mm film, courtesy Randy Sheets.

Still photo taken from 8mm film, courtesy Randy Sheets.

Photo by Patricia Salamone

Mom and child in concession area.

Hog Farmer Jean Nichols recalls, "Early on, we were doing things to engage the people that were showing up, getting them to help. I remember having a bonfire one night and trying to make the world's biggest marshmallow on a snow shovel by melting bags of marshmallows together. Everyone just went for that."

"Wine bottles and joints made the rounds as we sat and enjoyed the varied company and listened to the music," remembers Randy Sheets. "There was also a handful of little kids running around in various stages of undress— some naked, some with just a shirt. There was a real feeling of camaraderie and fun. Everyone was out to enjoy and have a peaceful time, and this feeling would pervade my entire Woodstock experience. We hung out there until early evening and then walked back to our spot in front of the stage and watched as final preparations were made with lighting, sound, and completing the setup of the stage. This was only Wednesday, so final setup was in full swing.

"As it got dark, we figured it would be a good idea to find our campsite, which we managed, and folks were still sitting around their sites playing guitar and sharing what they had. One in our group found a long tree branch and rigged up the British flag that my brother had brought along, and that stood over our site. My brother, Scott, was into the British bands and everything British. We made some Goober sandwiches and slept, crowded into our tent.

"The next day, Thursday, was much the same—hanging out and grooving on the scene," Sheets continues. "We actually got up that morning and made blueberry pancakes on our Coleman stove! The blueberries were picked from some bushes that surrounded our meadow, and someone had brought boxed pancake mix. Our pancakes stuck without any oil, but we didn't care. They were so good!"

Still photo taken from 8mm film, courtesy Randy Sheets.

"Hoisting our flag," says Randy Sheets.

Still photo taken from 8mm film, courtesy Randy Sheets.

Blueberry pancakes.

I remember having a bonfire one night and trying to make the world's biggest marshmallow on a snow shovel by melting bags of marshmallows together.

Traffic on Route 17B.

Traffic on Route 17B.

Photos taken by George David Stelnik, photos courtesy of Debbie Stelnik.

Debbie Stelnik today.

White Lake local Debbie Stelnik recalls, "I was 11 and staying at a bungalow colony off 17B with my parents and sister. We were in the woods within walking distance from White Lake, right in the midst of all the people trying to find their way to the grounds. I remember the adults were scared, including my mom. Sure, we were used to a lot of middle-class urbanites traveling to the area for the summer, but nobody had ever seen anything like this. This was a relatively quiet place, and then all of a sudden here are all these people just walking through everyone's property. People were looking for food, water, or a place to sleep. A couple from Poland owned the colony, and they were absolutely freaking out. At night they stood guard with shotguns. The traffic was so incredible and my dad wanted to take a look, so we filled some water jugs and Dad passed it out as we went along. Everyone was so grateful, saying, 'Peace, man. Thanks.'"

Photo by Cornelius Alexy

Campers take over the adjacent fields.

By Thursday afternoon, Aug. 14, Woodstock was an idyllic commune of 25,000 people. The Hog Farmers had built kitchens and shelters with two-by-fours and tarps. Their kids were swinging on monkey bars built from lumber and tree limbs, jumping into the hay below. Wavy Gravy recruited responsible-looking people and made them security guards. He handed out armbands and revealed that the secret backstage password was "I forget."

Twenty-three-year-old Alan Futrell of Sanford, Florida, was ex-military and involved in the antiwar movement. He met a few people who were talking about the event, and though he wasn't one for concerts, he decided to hitch up and see if he could get in.

"I arrived on Thursday, and everyone was working frantically to get the stage and sound system finished," Futrell remembers. "I camped on the hill near the buses and volunteered to help the crew keep the place clean, just so I could get in.

"People were camped everywhere, a mass of tents and shelters. I spent much of my days roaming around, and I'd go back to the buses at night. I had a small backpack, and what I found was that I could actually leave it lay anywhere and not worry about anyone stealing; no one touched anyone's stuff. That was one of the main impressions I had—no worries.

"There was always some kind of food available. There were certain areas where you needed to buy it, but you really didn't need money, most of the people just welcomed you in. Whatever you needed seemed to be available through the people. It was very much communal living in the hippie sense."

"The stage was still being completed and there had to be thousands of people there already," recalls Greg Henry. "We were in the middle of the field while they were putting up a fence all around us. We fell asleep, and when we woke up, the fence was gone."

Chapter 2

PLEASE WALK ON THE GRASS

DAY ONE – FRIDAY, AUG. 15, 1969

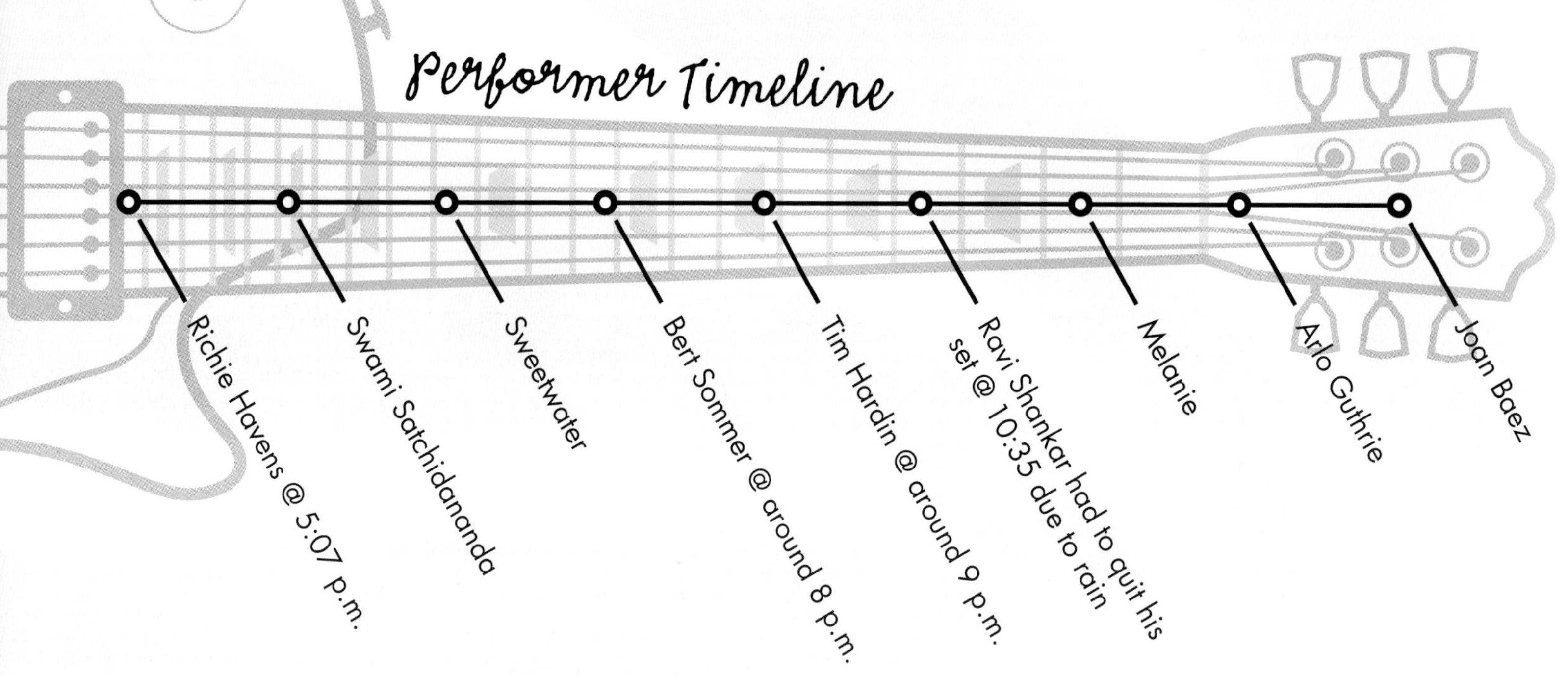

Photo by Dr. Bob Hieronimus

Bob Grimm with "Light" and a painted Volkswagen Bug.

"We're going camping!" That's what Tommy Hayes, 16, of Saddle Brook, New Jersey, told his parents, but he didn't tell them exactly where because he wasn't sure if they would have approved. He hitched a ride with some older friends, and his Woodstock adventure had began.

Trudy Morgal, 23, was the drummer in a house band called Light. They worked six nights a week and were never free to go to shows when bands came to town.

"Our friends would come by and tell us who they just saw, and we'd be like, 'God damn it. We don't ever get to see any-body.'" Her friend, Bob Grimm, had a bus, also named "Light," and artist Bob Hieronimus covered it with painted flowers and symbols to create the aura of the bus and what was representa-tive of the time. "When we heard about Woodstock, it was exciting to learn how many people were expected, and with the impressive lineup including so many of the greats, why wouldn't you go? So we took a week off from work."

Photo by Robin Chanin

The Chanins: Marc, 21; Lynn, 15; Michael, 17; and twin sister Robin, 17 (in scarf).

Seventeen-year-old Robin Chanin remembers seeing the poster with the dove and guitar. The festival's energy was simply omnipresent in their world. Chanin and her siblings Marc, Michael, and Lynn piled into her brother's '67 Ford Galaxy 500 convertible and headed for Bethel.

"We borrowed sleeping bags from our neighbors," Chanin recalls. "We didn't even have backpacks, so we didn't take a thing. No food or clothes. We were the kids from suburban Fords, New Jersey, who never camped a day in our lives."

"What a drag," remembers John Rossi, 18. "My mom didn't want us hitchhiking and insisted on giving my friend and me a ride to the Greyhound station to make sure we boarded the bus. We left Providence, Rhode Island, heading for New York City at about 8 a.m. on Friday morning. As it turned out, the bus was an excellent idea. When we got to the city we had to connect with another bus headed to White Lake. Well, we found ourselves 'at home.' The bus was filled with freaks—50 of our best friends we'd never met before—all heading to the same festival together, rapping and sharing all the way."

Linda Breslin of Boston was 18. She and her husband, Jim, planned on hitchhiking, but found out that their neighbor and his girlfriend were going, too, so they caught a ride with them. "Jim and I didn't go prepared with anything, but I remember our friends had a cooler with some food and a bottle of wine. We left on Friday in his van with shag carpeting."

Photo by Jim and Linda Breslin

Linda Breslin on the way to Woodstock.

The bus was filled with freaks—50 of our best friends we'd never met before—all heading to the same festival together, rapping and sharing all the way.

Producer Michael Lang woke up Friday morning to realize that something was missing…the ticket booths. Others had known for days, but Lang said that morning was his first inkling that Woodstock would never collect a single dollar at the gate.

"By then, the main road leading in had become the busiest two-lane highway in America as everybody converged for one big cosmic, cultural celebration. Signs read 'Welcome Aquarians' and it looked like the entire Aquarian Nation was marching past. The multiple lanes of traffic heading west ground to a halt, and the roadsides became littered with abandoned vehicles. People found it easier to proceed on foot and joined the mass heading down the road to the festival site," says Stu Fox of Ithaca, New York.

Courtesy Lynden Lilley, with special thanks to Ken VanLoan. Photo by Joanne Hague.

This peace sign and dove cut-out is an exact duplicate of the one originally handcrafted by Ken VanLoan using the top of a metal picnic table. It was seen by concert-goers on their way to the festival.

© Elliott Landy/Landyvision.com

Festival director Michael Lang in consultation on the stage.

Brooklyn residents Babette Brackett, 25, and her husband packed their Volkswagen square back sedan with two coolers full of food, two tents, ponchos, air mattresses, plastic shower curtains, a portable playpen-crib filled with baby toys, a bag of puzzles, crayons, books, and their two children—Anna was 3-1/2 and Nathan was 8 months.

"We left on Friday morning because rumors were circulating that 200,000 people might be there," recalls Brackett. "We passed a camper pulled over on the Thruway, and the state police were going through every piece of their baggage. After that we drove especially careful. It took about three hours to get to White Lake and more than an hour to travel the final three miles to Hurd Road."

Photo by Stephen Teso

Passing time in traffic.

Paul Lehrman was 16 at the time and attending high school on Long Island, New York. He bought advance tickets as soon as they came out, making him one of approximately 186,000.

"I hooked up with my friend Roger, who was a couple of years older than me and able to borrow his mom's Plymouth Valiant to get us there," Lehrman says. "Equipped with two sleeping bags, two rain ponchos, a couple of changes of underwear and a canned ham, we headed to Woodstock." Shortly after noon, they found themselves at a dead stop in traffic about 10 miles from the site. They spent the next several hours crawling along the back roads looking for the concert site.

Patricia Salamone from Hicksville, New York, was 18 when she heard about the Woodstock Festival, but it was the Arts Show and Crafts Bazaar that caught her eye. "I was doing a lot of crafts at the time and thought it would be a wonderful place to display my items." Little did she know that due to matters of organization and time constraints, the crafts fair, like the ticket booths, would not be there.

Photo by Stephen Teso

It was the busiest two-lane highway in America.

There were people camping and sitting all along the roadside, and I remember people jumping on our van just to catch a ride for the last couple of miles.

"At that time in my life, I was still going to church. I was Catholic, so before we left Friday morning, I went to mass knowing I would miss on Sunday," Salamone says. Not knowing what lay ahead, she laughs now as she remembers wanting to look just right at the festival. "All I took was clothes and make-up."

"As we got closer on 17B," Trudy Morgal says, "the police were stopping cars and questioning where you were going. If you said Woodstock, they wanted to see your tickets before they'd let you pass. There were people camping and sitting all along the roadside, and I remember people jumping on our van [Light] just to catch a ride for the last couple of miles."

Photo by Dr. Bob Hieronimus

"Light" was Trudy Morgal's home at Woodstock for the next three days.

Woodstock or Bust

Photo courtesy Cornelius Alexy

Camping at the side of the highway en route to Woodstock.

Photo courtesy Cornelius Alexy

Cars parked everywhere en route.

Photo courtesy Cornelius Alexy

Vehicles left abandoned along the road.

Photo courtesy Cornelius Alexy

Woodstock or bust.

Photo by Gary Geyer

Watchers, waders and those who bared all to cool off at Forsythia Cove.

Fete on Friday: Freedom, pot, skinny-dipping

By ETHEL G. ROMM

WHITE LAKE

A quarter of a million Baptists holding a convention on this site would be a problem and these are not Baptists.

They are having fun with all the forbidden pleasures from smoking you-know-what to skinny-dipping, (nude bathing) in the pond.

Mostly they are sitting around talking and laughing on blankets spread over 600 acres of countryside.

It has been a happy, very quiet place, a guitar picking out a tune here and there, a child swinging on a rope put up on a tree for him.

The scene is in sharp counterpoint to the frustration suffered by thousands of festival-goers unable to reach their destination.

At 4 p.m. everyone is waiting for the music to begin. They will wait more than an hour.

Someone is entertaining the crowd with Yoga exercises: "Take a deep breath and keep your spine very straight. That's where the main energy of your body goes."

The crowd doesn't know it but some vital parts for the sound system were just brought in by helicopter so it will be a while before the music begins.

The show is late, there are seven hours of travel for the last 15 miles, parking lots are five miles away, toilet facilities are overloaded and sanitation trucks can't get through.

The tribe has gathered -- the long-haired boy gypsies and their pretty "old ladies" in pilgrim dress. The hip students and the young rock rebels.

Because of the known traffic problems outside, those of us here feel we are in a special place. We also feel marooned, not sure the traffic will ever un-jam.

Actually, today's performance is free, and all the others probably will be. The fences were gently pushed down early in the day -- they had been carelessly installed. There is no way to charge anyone. No turnstiles to go through.

"Will someone throw me out?" asks one gate-crasher timidly of a guard.

Shopkeepers, in their colorful tents back in the woods, are delighted. "They'll have more money to spend here," one says.

Nobody is worried about the promoters. Depending on who is doing the talking, spokesmen say either 150,000 or 250,000 tickets have been sold. That should cover the expenses of turning this raw land into an entertainment site with electricity, water, telephones, and roads.

Much extra money is expected to come from a film being made about the festival, similar to the successful movie about Monterey.

Rumors fly quickly -- gypsy concessionaires sold out their ice cream and orangeades early and the word is out that food supplies were exhausted by mid morning.

Authorized food caterers are in their own section on a hill, prepared to feed 100,000 a day. If attendance guesses are accurate they may run short.

The Hog Farm commune, flown from their home base in New Mexico, has been serving brown rice and bean soup from open vats to youngsters who came without money. That word spread quickly.

Maybe there will be a riot today or tomorrow. Maybe it will all turn into a very bad scene. Maybe we'll all get dysentary or hepititis.

Right now we're at a happy carnival with young children cavorting through inventive playgrounds and older ones swaying to rock and folk music.

Photo by John De Lorenzo

"...Sitting around talking and laughing on blankets spread over 600 acres of countryside." From "Fete on Friday: Freedom, Pot, Skinning-Dipping," Times-Herald Record.

Victory at Woodstock.

Photo by Lee Levin-Friend

"We were stopped at a partially patched chain link gate by one of the off-duty New York City policemen that formed the festival security," recalls Babette Brackett. "He told us that we would have to leave our car and hike in. I knew that we couldn't schlep the kids and all our gear that last mile, so I picked up Nathan and pinched him to make him cry. The ruse worked and we drove to Filippini's Pond, the lake behind the main stage, where we pitched our tents about 100 feet from the water. Anna christened it 'Brown Lake' a day later after the first storm and several thousand bathers stirred up its bottom."

Fifteen-year-old Jeryl Abramson from Brooklyn was staying at a bungalow colony in August and recalls that "we were totally taken by surprise at what was happening when that weekend began. We had no TV, the phones were party lines so nobody could stay on them long, and we never even got a newspaper. We were very cloistered at the colony.

"When we awoke on Friday morning, there were thousands of people that weren't there the day before. That's when we found out about Woodstock. I remember my mother and I making peanut butter and jelly sandwiches and gathering up gallon jugs of water and taking them down to the median on Rt. 17 to give away. I remember seeing all the different license plates—Alaska, California, and Nevada. It was very exciting to me."

The concert bowl filling up.

Photo by David Marks (3rd Ear Music/Hidden Years Music Archives 1969-2009)

For Iris Shapiro of Long Island, Woodstock was her first taste of freedom. She and four friends from work got into their friend's big black Chrysler but soon found it faster to walk than drive. "It looked like a pilgrimage to Mecca," she says. "Everyone was heading in the same direction with various items of baggage. It was very hot and soon became clear that it was no short distance, but after a time we started seeing houses and the beginnings of some organized locale. Some residents being barraged by requests for water started selling the stuff by the glass, and to cool [off], pilgrims were stripping and jumping in residents' pools."

Photo by Lee Levin-Friend

Lee Levin-Friend's Pontiac GTO in White Lake. It was easier just to walk to the festival.

Lee Levin-Friend, 23, from Philadelphia, and her husband pulled into White Lake with her 1967 Pontiac GTO convertible on Friday about 8:30 a.m. and started following the crowd. "As we went through town, we weren't aware that even with plenty of money, there wouldn't be anything to buy except for five oranges. The town was sold out of everything. We also realized that we didn't have a place to stay for the weekend. I was four months pregnant with our first child, which meant that I had to use the restroom a lot. Of course there weren't any except for 'johnny on the spot' and there weren't many of those, either. So here we were, totally unprepared for what we knew was something very exciting and magnetic."

"Everyone looked just like us," remembers Robin Chanin. "It was a great equalizer. No one stood out. There was a moving river of blue jeans and flowing hair, lots of beads, embroidery, and flowers. We parked our car in a field with others, and not knowing where to go, we joined the throng and the movement simply took us there."

Bob Grimm drove Light up the tree-lined dirt road to the festival grounds and found a place to park near the portable toilets on the hill to the left. This was to be their home for the next three days. "At that time, the crowd was filling the bowl," says Trudy Morgal. "As people came in they got close to the stage, and the mass built from there back."

Ken Babbs [of the Merry Pranksters] and Wavy Gravy watched as a dozen guys in orange jackets walked up the rise. They were the ticket-takers. To accomplish that task, they wanted everyone already there to walk out and then come back in. Babbs said, "Man, you gotta be kidding me. There are 200,000 people in there." The head security man agreed that there was no way possible to collect all the tickets, and he asked what we wanted to do.

Photo courtesy Associated Press

Trudy Morgal and friend Rick Peters on top of Light.

Photo by Jim and Linda Breslin

Shoulder to shoulder waiting for the music.

"They had a double-wide section of fence that was open for the gate," Babbs recalls. "Wavy and I said the only thing to do is take it down. So we [Wavy and I] unrolled the fence about a hundred feet, and the people came pouring in."

The huge stage looked like a small city, and the performers and techs like scurrying insects.

Photo by Cornelius Alexy

The crew on stage with the crowd waiting.

There was a moving river of blue jeans and flowing hair, lots of beads, embroidery, and flowers.

"It was pretty crazy," remembers Trudy Morgal. "What were they thinking? The people in charge, I mean. If you look at the tickets, they were day passes. I've always wondered what they were going to do. Were they going to run everybody out of there on Friday night and tell them to come back Saturday? I'd hate to think that the event was ill planned and something that had gotten so big that it wasn't well thought out. But I believe if everything had been well planned, it would have been extremely chaotic."

Photo by Patrick Howe

Patrick Howe's view of the stage.

Elliot Tiber wrote in his published article, "How Woodstock Happened," that Michael Lang said he never exactly made the decision that Woodstock would become a free show, but he did decide to make the announcement. "It was kind of like stating the obvious," he said.

Patrick Howe was 19 and living in Toledo, Ohio, when he learned about Woodstock. "My friend and I bought advance tickets, and we convinced two other friends to go along, figuring they could buy theirs when we got there. We took a tent and what looked like a lot of food and left for the concert. When we arrived, tickets were irrelevant. There weren't any ticket-takers and no one seemed to care. The site was beginning to fill up, and we pitched our tent at the top of the hill. We watched them finish building the stage and set up the sound system."

Photos by Patrick Howe

Patrick Howe, 19. Patrick Howe's campsite.

Photo by Cornelius Alexy

The enormous stage had its own elevator for equipment.

When we arrived, tickets were irrelevant.
There weren't any ticket-takers
and no one seemed to care.

Photo courtesy Clay Borris/www.johnphillipsphotography.com

Friday's crowd keeps growing.

It was a sea of people, filling the hillside in bright colors, freaky clothes, and the freak-flag itself. Long, wild hair that usually earned a hostile or sarcastic stare everywhere else was like a badge of honor here."

Photos by Patrick Howe

Photos by Patrick Howe

Photos by Patrick Howe

Photo by Lee Levin-Friend

Friday in the concert bowl.

Caleb Rossiter, 17, of Ithaca, New York, rode his Triumph 500 down the county road between miles of backed-up cars. On that first afternoon he recalls, "The crowd was amazed and heartened by its own size as it flowed toward the farm. But only when we came up to the ridge that looked over the long slope down to the stage did the shock set in. People first murmured in awe and then roared with approval. It was a sea of people, like you and with you, filling the hillside in bright colors, freaky clothes, and the freak-flag itself. Long, wild hair that usually earned a hostile or sarcastic stare everywhere else was like a badge of honor here."

"After several hours of a slow crawl, we were waved off the dirt road by someone looking vaguely official and directed into a field where we would park," remembers Paul Lehrman. "As we walked, we began to hear a kind of roar in the distance. We came over a ridge and found ourselves at the edge of what could only be described as a sea of humanity. The scale of it was hard to believe. The huge stage looked like a small city, and the performers and techs like scurrying insects. The perimeter of the natural amphitheater was lined with porta-sans, and way off in the distance were cone-roofed tents surrounded by hordes of people, which we thought must be where the food was. Everyone was seated on blankets, straw mats, their jackets, or just in the grass."

Photo by John De Lorenzo

Getting through the crowd.

Photo by John De Lorenzo

Goin' up the country.

Photo by Derek Redmond and Paul Campbell

They came from all over the world.

Photo by Christopher Cole

Christopher Cole rode this bike to Woodstock.

Christopher Cole, 20, of Tarrytown, New York, left for Bethel with Maria, the girl he'd met the day before, and a duffle bag strapped to the sissy bar of his motorcycle. "As we approached the rim of the natural amphitheater, the hillside was filled with spectators, and I gazed on the stage down below. Just then the sun peaked from behind the clouds and the moment crystallized as I stood there with this beautiful young girl, a bottle of wine, and my motorcycle, in the midst of hundreds of thousands of young unsupervised kids my age. It just didn't get better than that! I looked up toward heaven and said, 'Thank you, God.'"

Photo by Derek Redmond and Paul Campbell

A view of the concert from the campground.

The morning of Aug. 15, 1969.

Photo by Christopher Cole

Christopher Cole getting ready to leave.

Photo by Christopher Cole

Christopher Cole with the girl he just couldn't leave at Woodstock.

Robin Chanin recalls, "The camaraderie reminded me of Walt Whitman's [words]: 'And what I assume, you shall assume; for every atom belonging to me, as good belongs to you.' It felt like we were all connected in the moment on the same path."

While the main stage was still being built, Babette Brackett, family, and friends went to the free stage. "We heard a rock band from Boston called Quarry, who was occasionally silenced by electrical failures, but nothing dampened the spirit of the communal love and anticipation that was building up," she says. "Whenever the generator was being fixed, we'd be amused by someone sending Roman candles and other fireworks into the sky."

Photo by Patricia Salamone

The crowd at Woodstock.

Photo by Jim and Linda Breslin

Jim and Linda Breslin's view looking up the hill.

Photo by Jackie Watkins

Jackie Watkins, 15.

By mid-day Friday, it was scorching and humid. Jackie Watkins, 11-1/2 hours from Sparta, Wisconsin, remembers that "the hardest thing was not having any shade. Unless you went back into the wooded areas where the encampments were, there wasn't any shade in the concert area. They tried to put up canopies, but they just blew down. It was hot and there was a ton of dust."

Iris Shapiro remembers clearly the numerous announcements coming from the stage: "Stay away from the brown acid, it's a bad trip" and "Bonnie needs her medicine, so if Bob could meet her at the phones...."

"We got hungry and went to the food trailers to get something to eat, but there wasn't anything at all! They hadn't anticipated the crowd and promised that more food had been sent for and told us to come back in a few hours. My stomach just growled," remembers Shapiro. "As we walked back to our spot on the hill, some Hare Krishnas offered us orange segments, which we gratefully accepted."

They arrive with fest tickets, little else

By EILEEN SIMAS and NANCY WHIPPLE

WHITE LAKE

A spoonful of pork 'n' beans. A peanut butter sandwich. Some unchilled wine. Even a puff of 'grass.'

Whatever they've got they'll share with you, or anyone who wants it.

This seems to be the pervasive philosophy at the campsites that ring the Aquarian Exposition site in White Lake.

A young man who quit his job in Clifton, N.J., to come to the festival sat atop his expensive convertible and treated several new acquaintances to lunch -- peanut butter and jelly on rye bread.

"I brought food along," he said, "and so long as I've got it, I'll share it. After mine gives out, I'll bum it." He added that at the rate he was going, it wouldn't last longer than an hour.

One of his companions, a college sophomore from Chicago, said he was starving. "I spent $1.50 for a sandwich yesterday in Monticello," he explained.

Drunk? No. Tired? Probably. Why? Because he came from a long way off to White Lake in Sullivan County to attend the Aquarian Festival, a three-day extravaganza of folk-rock music, art, and poetry in the open air. He's typical of thousands who got in early to rest, likely the last they'll get for almost 48 hours.--TH-Record photo

"That was all I had for food."

He had come to the festival with others, but he didn't know where they were. He had one small canvas bag with him, no money, and, at that moment, no place to sleep. But, he had gotten his tickets to the festival months ago.

That is the way it was with many of the young men and women this team of reporters met Thursday during a tour of the camps at White Lake. Often, they had little or no money; no sure means of transportation; and no idea of where the next meal was coming from. But, always, they had their festival tickets in hand.

Two teenagers, both male, had just arrived from Philadelphia, Pa. They had traveled by bus; hitchhiked and walked. They came to the festival site and pitched a tent. "I don't know how we're going to get home," one said. "It sure was expensive getting here."

What were they going to do about food? "I don't know," the other said. "We just won't eat for a couple of days."

Another group of college-age men had travelled from New Jersey. Thursday, seven of them were camping out in a Volkswagen bus.

"It's great," one said, offering a pot of pork 'n' beans around. "Two of us sleep on the top; two, inside; and three, outside." He added that nine more were expected by nightfall. "They're traveling all different ways to get here," he said.

In the afternoon sun, most guys and girls were just sitting around or sleeping. A few strummed guitars. One man passed out leaflets. Fires warmed canned goods, and car tops and stationwagon rears did double duty as table tops and chairs.

As if by some unspoken pre-arrangement, everyone seemed to be wearing the same thing. Boys: Stripped to the waist or sporting vests. Girls: Sans bras, for the most part, but concealing their bralessness under billowy tops. Both: Bell-bottom dungarees, and long hair.

There were few couples, married or otherwise. Most of the campers were groups of six or more young men or small communities of a dozen or more persons of both sexes. Boys outnumbered girls everywhere we visited.

Both refreshing and perplexing was the fact that no one seemed to worry, not about the future, not about the past, not even about today.

What are you doing about food? How are you going to get home? Where are you going? These were questions we asked. Over and over, the reply was the same: I don't know.

A little bit of caring was needed at the campsites. In the main areas, congested with people and tents, some were already strewing their discarded food containers about the grounds.

Roads were cluttered with young people on foot, and cars, campers, and workmen's equipment, all struggling to be on their way. The toilet facilities and the running water were far away from the campsites, perhaps accounting for the road congestion.

Two girls, barely out of high school, told us that Thursday morning they had eaten eggs and oatmeal free. "The festival is trying to feed all those who have no money," one girl said.

"They have one kitchen now and they're setting up another. And, water is being piped or trucked into the camps and there's work for everyone who wants to work," she added.

Some do provide for those who cannot.

It was hard to find food and water and, yes, toilet paper. We were able to buy five oranges from another concert-goer, but there was no food to buy from any of the concessions at the concert site.

Photo by Lee Levin-Friend

Lee Levin-Friend (in the yellow shirt) finds a spot at the crest of the concert bowl.

Still photo taken from 8mm film, courtesy Randy Sheets.

It was like gold.

Lee Levin-Friend recalls, "It was hard to find food and water and, yes, toilet paper. We were able to buy five oranges from another concert-goer, but there was no food to buy from any of the concessions at the concert site."

Stephen Teso, 16, of Worcester, Massachusetts, remembers learning of the Hog Farm. "They were set up and shoveling out large quantities of what may or may not have been oatmeal. But it was hot and it was good. Loudspeakers were telling us to be cool—the music would be starting soon."

Richie Havens arriving.

Photo by Cornelius Alexy

Photos by Cornelius Alexy

Photos by Cornelius Alexy

Kids waiting at Monticello Raceway to see their heroes.

Finally, around 5 o'clock, the first performer was announced. Howard Smead remembers, "We all stood up and cheered. Richie Havens was first and stood dreadfully alone on that giant stage. Havens was tall and somber, dressed in an African robe and missing lots of teeth. He was obviously over 30 but just as obviously someone to trust; a sympathetic but demanding teacher. He attacked his well-worn guitar and vocal cords, asking us:

> *'Hey, lookie yonder, tell me what's that you see, marching to the Korean War? Looks like handsome Johnny with his rifle in his hand....'"*

According to Smead, "It was Richie Havens and his first song, 'Handsome Johnny,' that crystallized the mood into a kind of celebration of defiance. We would triumph. Damn the war, damn the government, damn the politicians, and damn the weather. We were marching off to our own war."

Richie Havens remembers how he ended up going on stage first. "We were all seven miles away at two hotels, and there weren't any roads to get the entertainers or the equipment to the field," he says. "So there really wasn't going to be a Woodstock if they didn't get a helicopter to the Holiday Inn driveway. It just so happened that the first was a private helicopter, and having the least [amount of] instruments, we went over to the field first. I was supposed to be fifth on the bill," the folk singer recalls.

Photo by David Marks (3rd Ear Music/Hidden Years Music Archives 1969-2009)

Richie Havens.

Photo by Derek Redmond and Paul Campbell

Richie Havens performing for over three hours.

A round of applause for Richie Havens.

Photo by Derek Redmond and Paul Campbell

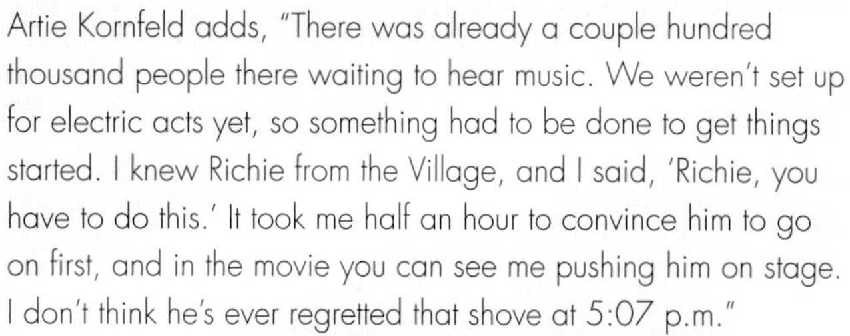

Artie Kornfeld adds, "There was already a couple hundred thousand people there waiting to hear music. We weren't set up for electric acts yet, so something had to be done to get things started. I knew Richie from the Village, and I said, 'Richie, you have to do this.' It took me half an hour to convince him to go on first, and in the movie you can see me pushing him on stage. I don't think he's ever regretted that shove at 5:07 p.m."

With Havens' welcome to the audience with "Clap your hands...clap your hands," Woodstock had begun. Havens played a lengthy set because the other musicians hadn't arrived yet, and after running through all of his material, he combined several songs and created the song, "Freedom."

"I didn't know his music very well," remembers Patricia Salamone, "but when he did 'Freedom,' everybody just went crazy."

Kornfeld continues: "After three hours, Richie left the stage, and we still weren't ready for a band. We needed another performer fast, and I knew John Sebastian was at the festival. Linda [my wife] and John were sitting under a tarpaulin together, and I went to John and asked him if he'd like to perform. John was not on the bill; he'd not been in front of a crowd for a year or performed any of his new solo material since the [Lovin'] Spoonful broke up, and he and my wife had just dropped acid.

With the highways jammed, there was only one way to transport supplies and performers.

Photos by Cornelius Alexy

Crew loading supplies for the festival onto a helicopter, while kids stop to hang out.

Photo by David Marks (3rd Ear Music/Hidden Years Music Archives 1969-2009)

John Sebastian, Woodstock's "unscheduled" great.

"John said, 'What do you mean, you want me to play? I can't go on. I have nothing prepared.' I said, 'John, you're as much a part of why we're doing this thing as anyone else. You need to go on.' We tried to get Tim Hardin to perform next but he was too scared, so I asked if I could borrow his guitar. John went on stage, forgot some words, but really came through. He became a real highlight of the show."

After John Sebastian, the search continued for the next act. Country Joe McDonald was scheduled to appear on Sunday, but he was also at the festival hanging out. "It never dawned on me that I would be asked to play," said McDonald. "I was stunned and made a lot of excuses not to do it. They found a guitar and tied a rope to it for a strap and pushed me out in front of the masses. When I walked on stage and saw the huge audience, it took my breath away for a moment. No one paid any attention to me."

The Earth Light folks (yellow loin cloths) entertain the crowd.

Photos by John De Lorenzo

Photo by David Marks (3rd Ear Music/Hidden Years Music Archives 1969-2009)

Casual and free.

And it's one, two, three, what are we fighting for
Don't ask me I don't give a damn, next stop is Vietnam
And it's five, six, seven, open up the pearly gates
Ain't no time to wonder why, whoopee, we're all gonna die.
—Country Joe McDonald

Most people on the hill didn't even realize McDonald was on stage until he went into the cheer: "Gimme an F, gimme a U, gimme a C, gimme a K!" The folks at the bottom of the hill picked it up first, and by the time he asked, "What's that spell?," a sea of people roared out the answer.

The audience came to life for a massive sing-along of the "I Feel-Like-I'm-Fixin'-To-Die-Rag," and Country Joe was totally drowned out.

As the performances continued, so did the influx of humanity. The bowl area continued to fill, as well as the surrounding areas.

"There really wasn't any way to police this thing. We had to take care of each other," says Trudy Morgal. "I would dare anybody to harass someone in that crowd the way everybody's head was. There were just too many people around. We needed to be our own security. You'd just need to say something like, 'Hey, man…be cool,' but I didn't even hear that."

Friday evolved into a day of celebration with the audience becoming the featured stars. The entire landscape was draped in a kaleidoscope of colors that sparkled in the sunshine; energy and excitement radiated throughout the site. It was a time of discovery and many people caught only bits and pieces of what was happening on the stage. Swami Satchidananda came out and spoke to the nation of young people.

Photo by Harriette Schwartz

"The future of the whole world is in your hands," he told them. "You can make it or you can break it. But you are really here to make the world, not to break it. There is a dynamic power here. Hearts are meeting."

Photo by Derek Redmond and Paul Campbell

Nancy Nevins and Sweetwater take the stage.

Nancy Nevins of Sweetwater remembers, "We were scheduled to open the show at noon, and we were way past time. We were the first band to be flown in by helicopter, and on their way to the site, Alex [our keyboardist] asked the pilot what all the crops were down below. 'Those are people, dude,' the pilot answered."

The sound system was definitely not ready for any band to play when Sweetwater took the stage. "The sound was awful when we went on," Nevins says. "There were no monitors, and everything, including drums, was recorded through the vocal mikes. My voice evaporated into the air once it left my throat. Worse, I couldn't hear the other singers, so we performed by memory alone. Fred [our bass player] claims Sweetwater was the sound check for Woodstock. In spite of it all, by the end of our set, we got the crowd on its feet, and like Richie and Joe before us, continued to connect with our songs. Sweetwater lit the fire for Woodstock."

What's wrong in our schools?
Politicians are blowing
their cools
Over they who refuse
to follow the rules
Though they should be
separate dealings
—Alex Del Zoppo (Sweetwater)

Lynn Spencer's view.

Photo by Lynn Spencer

Photo by John De Lorenzo

Moonfire makes Woodstock's messages many.

Photo by John De Lorenzo

Flying in supplies down the road from the concert bowl.

Ira Stone, Bert Sommer's lead guitarist, recalls, "We arrived in upstate New York on Thursday and hung out until Friday when we had to get to the festival. Our caravan of cars got caught in the traffic gridlock, so we had to wait in a field for a helicopter to fly us to the stage area. Can you imagine waiting in a field with [among others] the Maharishi, Tim Hardin, and Bert? Not too surreal! None of us realized the scope of this event until the chopper cleared the hillside. Then we were in awe! All we saw was an ocean of undulating colors. There were so many people, and a sight that we will never forget! We did the cover of [Simon and Garfunkel's] 'America' and got the first standing ovation of the Festival."

Photo by Stephen Teso

Stephen Teso gets up close with Moonfire.

Photo by Victor Kahn

Victor Kahn, Ira Stone, and Woodstock co-creator and promoter, Artie Kornfeld, today.

Stone remembers, "Actually, the funniest moment at the whole festival had to be when they stopped Bert's performance because of people climbing the towers. Warnings came from [lighting/staging director/emcee] Chip Monck that the show wouldn't continue until all the climbers came down. There were a few harsh words from those up there, but Bert replied to the crazy comments with a cute 'f___ you' over the PA system, and the entire festival roared their approval!" It was 8:20 p.m., just before sunset and the rain hadn't started to mist yet.

Photo by Victor Kahn

Ira Stone.

Still photo taken from 8mm film, courtesy Randy Sheets.

Getting a better view.

Photo by John De Lorenzo

Photo by Victor Kahn

Bert Sommer (left) shows Artie Kornfeld lyrics he wrote at Woodstock for "We're all playing in the same band."

When Tommy Hayes arrived in White Lake, he knew it was already late. "It was raining on and off all evening, and just when it started to pour, we came upon a barn. I remember everyone going in, so we followed. At that moment, I believe I was witnessing my first 'free love' experience. People were naked, up in the loft, drinking wine, playing around, and having a good time. I kept my clothes on and just went with the flow. We never made it to the concert Friday, but we did have a dry place for the night."

Howard Smead remembers that the rain held off until the very end of Ravi Shankar, and that it was Chip Monck who enabled everyone to endure the rain. "Chip had the kind of voice you'd want your father to have, very well modulated, very calm and knowing. Anyone who listened to him could not help but feel comforted, even as the rain pelted the festival without mercy."

Smead recalls, "Before the rain started on Friday night, Chip told us Tiny Tim had suggested that everyone in the audience light a match and hold it aloft. We scurried around borrowing and distributing matches, and on his count struck them and held them high. There must have been well over 200,000 of us by that time, enough to produce a shockingly brilliant glow that re-created 30 seconds of daylight. The delighted crowd showed its approval by erupting into a roar of self-congratulation. A thing of such spontaneous beauty was to be savored though it only lasted seconds. I didn't want it to happen again, ever. It couldn't. It was the first time I knew I was part of something that very few people would ever have the chance to experience. We all belonged."

The thunderstorms blew into Bethel Friday night, and the adverse weather conditions became part of the festival's lore. Folk singer Melanie [Safka] recalls, "I remember the hillside lighting up. It had just started to rain, and the announcer made a real inspirational announcement about people lighting their candles and keeping their spirits high. It was magical, and I wrote 'Candles in the Rain' because of it."

Photo courtesy Chipmonck Archives

Woodstock lighting/staging director Chip Monck at eight years of age in 1948.

Photo courtesy Chipmonck Archives

Chip Monck directing "follow" spotlights during a concert in the United Kingdom in 1970.

E.H.B. (Chip) Monck has been behind the scenes of every major pop-culture event of the last 50 years, from The Village Gate in the early 1960s, the Apollo in Harlem, Newport with Dylan, lighting designer and emcee at Woodstock, losing teeth at Altamont at the hand of a Hells Angel's pool cue, the Stones' early tours, George Harrison's Concert for Bangladesh, Ali-Foreman's Rumble in the Jungle, "The Rocky Horror Show" on Broadway, and the Los Angeles Olympics to Pope John Paul at Dodger Stadium. Today, Chip Monck is as busy as ever, providing lighting design for major corporate clients from his home in Australia. His website is www.chipmonck.com.

Photo by John De Lorenzo

John De Lorenzo, 1969.

Photo by John De Lorenzo

Joe Duffy, friend of John De Lorenzo.

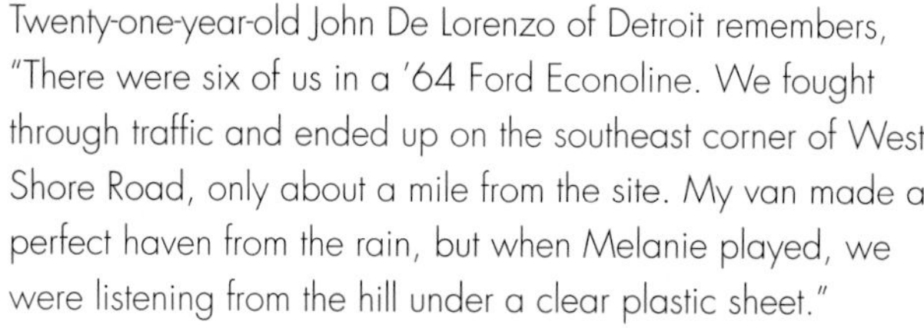

Twenty-one-year-old John De Lorenzo of Detroit remembers, "There were six of us in a '64 Ford Econoline. We fought through traffic and ended up on the southeast corner of West Shore Road, only about a mile from the site. My van made a perfect haven from the rain, but when Melanie played, we were listening from the hill under a clear plastic sheet."

"We sat in the drizzle for quite a while, but when it started raining harder, a huge 30-foot-long plastic tarp unfolded on top of our heads. Someone either planned for the rain or swiped it from somewhere. There were about a hundred of us sitting underneath that, holding it up with our hands," adds Gary Geyer.

Photo by John De Lorenzo

John Hartwig, friend of John De Lorenzo, resting by nearby White Lake.

"When the rain came in on Friday, it was really nice," remembers Patricia Salamone. "After being so hot, it cooled everything down, and we stayed out in the open for the night." She remembers many people, much like herself, who weren't prepared. "I had a backpack with me, with some clothes and my makeup. My only concern was looking good."

Linda Breslin remembers that it was raining when they arrived late Friday evening. "We heard on the radio that Woodstock had been declared a disaster area, so the first thing I did when I got there was find a pay phone and call home. My mother asked if I was aware what the news was reporting, but to me, it didn't seem that way at all. It was quite calm. The ground was muddy, but we made due with plastic bags to sit on."

Arlo Guthrie elated people's spirits with his stories between songs and helped wash away any discomfort the showers had brought. Richard Younger was a 15-year-old rock and roll addict from Brooklyn and recalls arriving at the crest of the hill where he could see Guthrie on the distant stage and hear the unmistakable "Comin' into Los Angeles. Bringin' in a couple of keys. Don't touch my bags if you please, Mr. Customs man."

"There were people and small campfires as far as one could see," Younger says. "Arlo told the crowd that the New York State freeway was closed. Something amazing was happening."

Joan Baez, pregnant and with her husband, David, in prison for resisting the draft, closed things out Friday with a highly charged political theme. Stu Fox remembers that people linked arms with strangers and swayed back and forth, singing along as she delivered the civil rights anthem "We Shall Overcome."

Milton Sirota, of Long Island, ran Camp Ma-Ho-Ge at Happy Avenue and Laymon Road, about a mile away. He remembers how the campers sat on the basketball court at night and listened to the music coming right over the mountain. Rich Klein was eight years old and clearly remembers that night. He thought the sweet sounds of Joan Baez were coming from the heavens.

Still photo taken from 8mm film, courtesy Randy Sheets.

The sound towers at dusk.

There were people and small campfires as far as one could see.

Photo by Cornelius Alexy

Chapter 3

"WHAT WE HAVE IN MIND IS BREAKFAST IN BED FOR 400,000."—WAVY GRAVY

DAY TWO – SATURDAY, AUG. 16, 1969

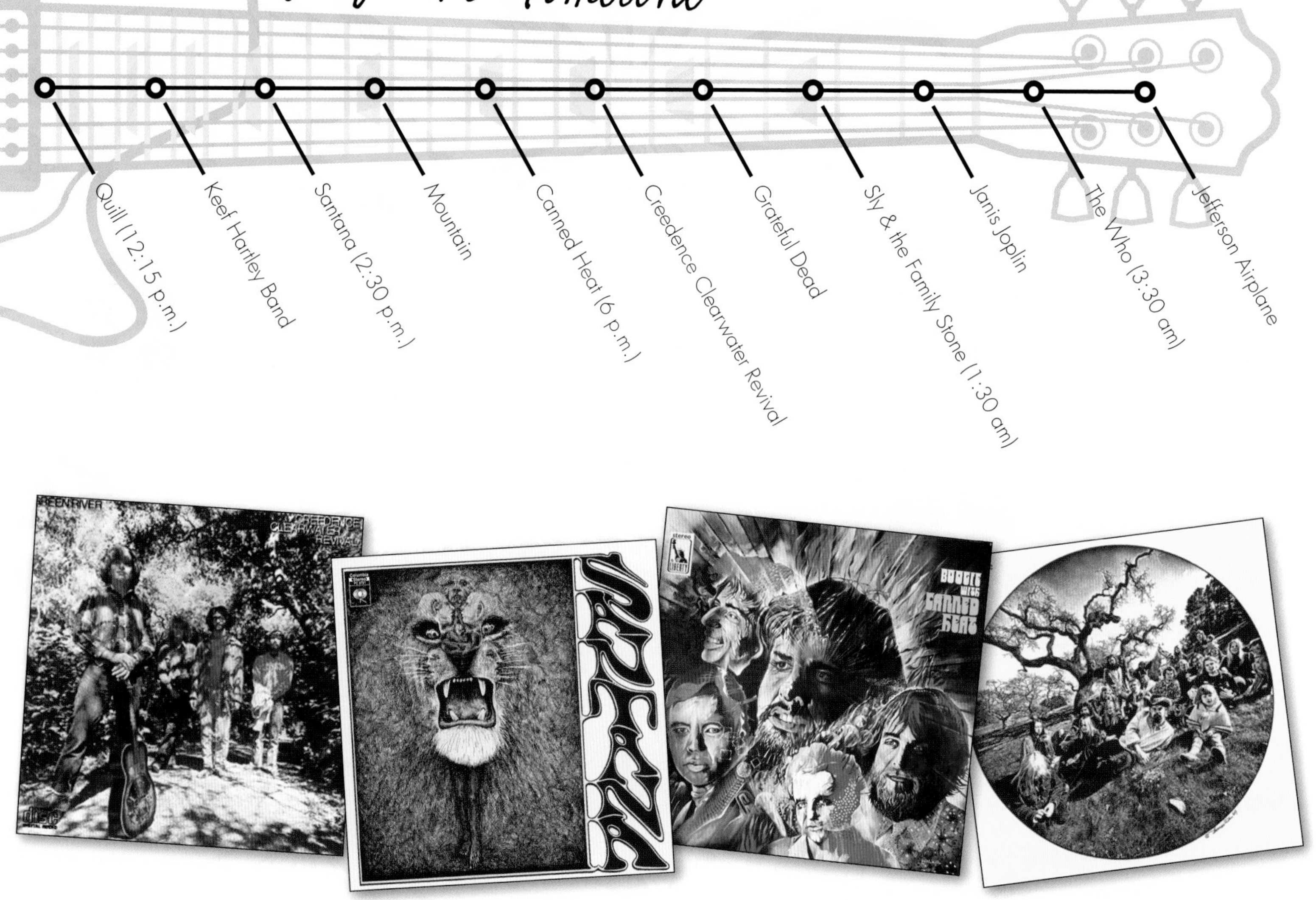

Photo by Stephen Teso

All roads lead to Woodstock.

Saturday morning dawned soggy and gray, and Michael Launder, 17, from Albion, New York, and his friend, Billy, hitched a ride on the trunk of a car covered in people. "There were about eight guys inside and another five or six sitting on the hood and trunk, so we just jumped on," says Launder. "When we finally reached the festival, it was very surprising to see the state troopers with their 'Smokey' hats off, hanging with the rest of us."

Smokeys keeping the peace—and their cool.

Still photo taken from 8mm film, courtesy Randy Sheets.

THE TIMES HERALD RECORD Saturday, August 16, 1969 3

200,000 at festival jam Sullivan highways

By FRED GERMAIN

WHITE LAKE

"Every kid in the world is here "

It's with superlatives like that that the opening of the three-day Aquarian Festival must be told -- the stars of the rock-folk heaven, a hip city of 200,000, and the most monumental traffic jam in the region's history

"Something snapped Something happened Every kid in the world is here "

Amidst a tent city with a population like that of Orange County and the problems of New York City, a festival official surveyed the agony and the ecstacy:

Agony that began Thursday when New York City said its off-duty police could not act as security men and the battle of the roads was lost.

Ecstacy at 5:07 when Richie Havens began to slam it out from a nearly completed stage before probably the largest crowd that ever sat on the grass -- many of them smoking same -- let the wind blow through its hair, and said to hell with conventions and the everyday world, let's hear music

Here are the highlights:

— The festival is on What they said couldn't be done has been The accomodations aren't the Waldorf, so first class means you've got water and toilet paper

— Outside the gate and along miles and miles of road leading to the 600-acre Bethel farm, it's a different story Traffic problems at the show billed as "Three Days of Peace and Music" will be a primer for a book on crowd control for the troopers, sheriff's men and others who faced the mobile onslaughts of free-wheeling youth from the middle of the week to 5:07 and beyond

— Aquarian's backers, according to two reports, were losing money John Morris, the official who saw "every kid in the world" before him, said $1 7 million had been spent by Friday and only $1 3 million collected

— The prospects for today are anyone's guess

"I'd like to do another festival," operations director Morris said, "but it would have to be in the Grand Canyon "

Stanley Goldstein, the show's assistant producer, put it another way -- "When we lost the cops, we lost the road When we lost the roads, we lost control of the traffic

"When that happened, we lost our supply lines "

And supply, as any West Point officer knows, is basic to any army, which is what this band of hippies is -- down to their uniforms

Trucks for concessionaires supplying thirsty thousands and the hundred and one other things an army needs fitfully integrated themselves into the long line of cars and pedestrians inching toward the festival

Once seeing the traffic -- or worse having driven in it -- you had to be amazed that anything came off at all.

Much of the individual successes and failures hinged on the initiative of state police and citizens' band radio operators

At any given hour throughout the day you could find another major problem An accident here. A foot run over there An arrest somewhere else

At any hour you could find people enjoying themselves despite all of it

At one tent -- one of thousands -- two youngsters groused to newsmen -- "We've got no water Nothing The toilets stink and there's no paper "

A third shows up carrying cow corn wrapped in an army jacket and swiped from a farmer's field

"How do you cook this stuff," they asked, not knowing what they had was a far cry from what the Jolly Green Giant puts in cans

Fifty yards away, over tent lines and prostrate bodies, was another tent Six youngsters sat on the grass and waited for 5:07

The six kids, including one from Chicago and one from the Bronx, whom you could tell apart in the dark by their accents were doing fine

They'd gotten out of their sleeping bags early in the day and walked -- and walked -- to Monticello for provisions. They had distilled water, and baked beans

Initiative spelled the difference between the two tents What the dry kids didn't know at the first tent was that there was a tankerful of water less than a half-mile away

Aquarian backers, staggered by the loss of private police and twice the crowd expected, were showing signs of the same initiative

Aquarian leaders, according to a prediction of one underground editor, were looking beyond the possibility of this year's red ink to a more successful operation next year

This version was easy to credit Friday The gate was non-existent and no attempt was made to take or check tickets It simply couldn't have been done

Morris said some attempt to check tickets would be made today

Greenberg terms festival 'disaster'

MONTICELLO

The president of Monticello Raceway in Aquarian Expo-torn Sullivan County promised to demand a full scale investigation of what he called the "disaster and abortion" of the rock festival

Leon Greenberg stated that all the business people of the county would join him in the demand, "except those who made a killing in exploiting some pathetic souls

"It's a sham when all this county can accomplish is announcements on radio and TV to stay out of our area," Greenberg said

He urged Sullivan taxpayers to demand that those responsible for "the mismanagement" should be taken to task "as soon as this holocaust is over "

Greenberg congratulated the people of Wallkill for showing the foresight and community pride to assume the position they have taken

Stating that attendance at the raceway was not seriously affected because of the festival, Greenberg said that the litter on Sullivan County roads and highways hurt him as a member of the community

"My major complaint is just gross mismanagement," he said -- "it looks like a war hit here "

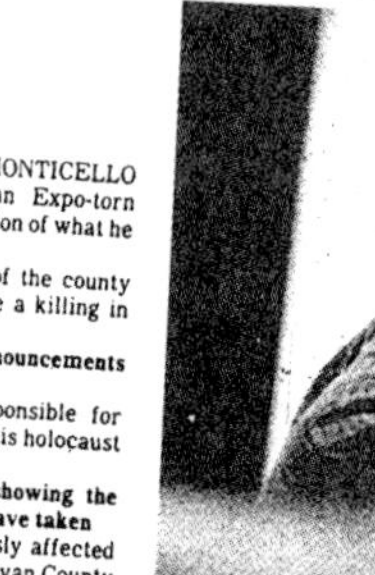

--TH-Record photo by Mike Lee

Singer-guitarist Richie Havens was opening performer at the Aquarian Festival in White Lake Friday afternoon. The artist was more than an hour late getting to the stage as an estimated 200,000 young people used every access road trying to get to the festival. Only about half made it within sight of the stage

Rockland mounties help

By DENIS THOET

WHITE LAKE

If there's a riot, or a fire, there's not much at all we can do We can't move anyone in and out in a hurry," said a mounted policeman from Rockland County

He was a part of a contingent of 20 sent from the county by agreement with the Sullivan County sheriff's office Although it was nearly impossible to learn what the actual security situation was at the exposition, it was reported that some off-duty policemen from New York City have ignored Police Commissioner Howard Leary's ban and are working, though without giving their names or job background

The mounted policeman said that "if we had been told to come yesterday, we could have prevented all this "

Movement on all access roads was virtually at a standstill Friday Ambulances had to fight their way through, moving at a rate of not more than 10 miles an hour

Traffic officials blink at other crises

By GIL WEISINGER

MONTICELLO

Sullivan County authorities, snowed under by a massive traffic problem, apparently took a "hands off" attitude Friday toward food, water, and other assistance for 200,000-plus festival patrons

A civil defense office spokesman in Monticello, when asked what provisions he was making for the increasing emergency, said tersely "None "

The office closed shortly after 2 Friday, but was reopened by several concerned citizens led by a Monticello resident, Jeffrey Blumenfeld

Blumenfeld and his associates kept lines of communication open to the site by employing citizens' band radios in CD headquarters. They were still toiling late Friday night, transmitting traffic reports whenever necessary

A sheriff's department spokesman said Sheriff Louis Ratner was handling traffic problems, the major cause of the "disaster," but was taking no special measures to provide food or water to the stranded

There were several unconfirmed reports of price gouging by stores and Bethel residents, with water said to be going for 25 cents a glass, bread and milk for $1 a loaf and quart, and other items scarce or completely unavailable, including gasoline

Elfenbaum's Delicatessin in Kauneonga Lake reported a "very serious" food supply situation. If no deliveries are made by today, a store employe said, "we will have to close our doors."

The employe said the store operates its own dairy but it took their truck six hours to deliver milk along a two-mile route Traffic, she noted, was at a "standstill" in Kauneonga Lake and cars were being abandoned in her area

Town magistrates were doing a brisk business with 51 arrests for narcotics violations reported by early Friday afternoon -- making the two day period -- Thursday and Friday -- the largest drug arrest period in Sullivan County history

Some magistrates were setting bail at $1,000 for possession of drugs and $10,000 for sale of narcotics and others were reported setting even higher bails for suspects

About 7:30 Friday night, the Monticello Fire Department dispatched a tank truck with water for the festival site where water was reported at a premium

Monticello firemen, hampered by heavy traffic, were kept busy late Thursday and early Friday with two fires at the Diamond Horseshoe Hotel on Rt 17B, major access route to the festival

The hotel, housing some 125 festival employes, was like a scene from the days of the pioneers Thursday as bucket brigade and hand-fire extinguishers, manned by hippie festival people, saved the hotel from a major disaster

Friday, another blaze broke out at the hotel, severely damaging two guest rooms and the second fire caused state police and local authorities to term the fires suspicious

Photo by John De Lorenzo

Anyone seen our tent?

Tommy Hayes made his way through fields and over downed fences following the crowd. The largest audience he'd ever been part of was at Madison Square Garden, and he had no idea how big *this* crowd could be; he just knew that it was a whole lot of people. "There were still some grassy areas in the field, so we found a spot and sat down. People were passing around pot and wine, and I was getting comfortable, digging on the music."

Area couple Nick Ercoline of Middletown, New York, and Bobbi Kelly of Pine Bush, both 20, were aware of all the Woodstock happenings through local newspapers, but never actually planned on going.

Linda and Jim Breslin's happy van driver.

Photo by Jim and Linda Breslin

Stay away from the brown acid.

Photo by Gary Geyer

"It wasn't until Friday night when we heard on the radio that 'if you're planning on going to Woodstock, do not come. The New York State Thruway is closed,' that we decided, with a few friends, that we just had to go check it out," says Kelly. "We were familiar with the area and took the back way, and when we reached standstill traffic, we followed a motorcycle through some fields to get closer as our big '65 Chevy station wagon bottomed out, front and back. When we couldn't drive any farther, we parked and immediately noticed that something was very wrong. A state trooper was standing next to his car and a young fellow was sitting on the hood smoking a joint. As we walked by, we heard him offer the trooper a drag and officer re-

Photo by Lee Levin-Friend

Walking to the festival.

Photo by Jim and Linda Breslin

Catching the vibe.

'If you're planning on going to Woodstock, do not come. The New York State Thruway is closed.'

plied, 'No, I don't indulge,' and he kept staring straight ahead. We thought, 'What the hell is this?' As we made our way closer to the festival site, we came upon Herbie, a young man from Huntington Beach, California, who lost the group he came with and was tripping out of his mind. He was alone so we brought him along with us. Herbie walked with his mighty staff—a pole with a butterfly on top. Herbie, if you're out there...."

John De Lorenzo decided to go wash in nearby Pucky's Pond but found it was full of moss. "Someone told me about a fresh water lake down on Hurd Road. As we made our way there, some of the locals were in their front yards being negative. They were blaming us for 'ruining everything,' but to the contrary, these very same people were offering us food and water on our way back—that's when my Woodstock epiphany began."

Photo by John De Lorenzo

John De Lorenzo sees others trying to bath at Pucky's Pond.

Photo by John De Lorenzo

Huddled on the hill.

Joanne Wilson Kelly today.

Joanne Wilson Kelly, 18, of Staten Island, New York, says, "It was a sea of people. I realized *this* was a big deal when I heard the announcements saying the Thruway was closed." She remembers that the view was exceptional from anywhere in the bowl and recalls her biggest problem was the far distance to the bathrooms. "There was just no way I could make it, so I used a cup. With all the naked people around me, I was sure I wasn't going to shock anyone."

Babette Brackett made blueberry pancakes. She fed her family and many others until the batter was gone. "A guy came by with a gallon of milk insisting that our kids might need it later," she remembers.

Camping near Filippini's Pond behind the stage area.

Photo by Lynn Spencer

Randy Sheets and friends walking down Hurd Road.

Still photo taken from 8mm film, courtesy Randy Sheets.

Trudy Morgal went out amongst the masses to get water for her friends. "I filled the jug but on the way back, people were like, 'Oh, man. Is that water?' 'Oh, can I...' and I was giving drinks to everyone. By the time I got back, I had none left. Everyone just looked at me and asked, 'Where's the water?' and I told them they'd have to get their own. There wasn't any way I could deny those people. I couldn't turn anybody down. I mean, I didn't want to. They were all hot just sitting there, and when you have a chance to get somebody something that they need, you do it. We were all there to help each other."

Robin Chanin's older brother left for several hours in search of food, and returned with a dozen hamburgers and a good-sized box of big soft pretzels someone gave him along the road. "We shared the bounty with our neighbors."

Photo courtesy Peter J. Corrigan, www.vintagerockandrollphotos.com

A gathering of epic proportion on Saturday.

Wavy Gravy (at microphone) plans breakfast in bed for 400,000.

Still photo taken from 8mm film, courtesy Randy Sheets.

Photo by Harriette Schwartz

Lineups for water.

"We brought food but it didn't last long and we didn't care," remembers Morgal. "We were really having a great time. All of us were in the exact same situation, so if you saw somebody with kids, you gave them what you had. You could last a day or two. We did get some watermelon at one of the booths, and Rick [our hippie Mr. Clean] asked for some napkins. The guy just looked at him like he was crazy; he wiped his own hands on his chest and said 'Yeah, like this.'"

After Friday, the concessions were out of food, so Lisa Law and the Hog Farm responded to the need. "Wavy [Gravy] got up on stage and declared, 'What we have in mind is breakfast in bed for 400,000,'" Lisa remembers. "That was the moment we started serving paper cups full of granola to the people in front of the stage. At one point I got hold of the stage mike and explained that if people would walk though the forest where the arts and crafts booths were [supposed to be], they could join the lines being served hot food by the Farmers. Tom [my husband] gasped and couldn't believe I'd just said that. He envisioned the entire gathering all getting up at the same time."

"We had open flames and were toasting oats using big stainless steel pots and pans, but soon that became hopeless," remembers Jahanara. "We brought a ton of vegetables with us that we were serving sautéed from the beginning, but there wasn't time for that either, and by Saturday we couldn't get to Yasgur's dairy store anymore. You couldn't get anywhere, so we cooked the bulgur and started dishing out sliced raw vegetables on the wheat and raw oats with honey and powdered milk on top.

Wavy got up on stage and declared, 'What we have in mind is breakfast in bed for 400,000.'

Photo by Gary Geyer

Shelter from the sun and storms.

Photo by Harriette Schwartz

"People would come and get their bowls of bulgur and then reach for the milk. This made the line move slowly. I realized it would be easier if I grabbed the milk and bowls and passed this out as I went down the line. Now, people had their bowls ready, just needing the wheat. It worked like a charm. Soon, another communal group from New York joined us. They were tough and competent just like us, and they blended right in. There were really efficient people working in the kitchen, and after a while it was operating very smoothly with food being turned out quickly. The National Guard dropped supplies, and whatever was brought in we used, however, the helicopters couldn't find a place to land. Campground supervisor Stanley Goldstein announced that sandwiches were coming into the Hog Farm compound by National Guard helicopter. Two hundred people created a landing pad by joining hands and forming a circle."

© Lisa Law Archives 1969

Hog Farm Free kitchen.

THE TIMES HERALD RECORD Saturday, August 16, 1969 9

From afar they came to walk on blistered feet

By MANNY FUCHS

They came from all directions in all kinds of vehicles, from shiny limousines to psychedelically-painted trucks of ancient vintage, from high-powered motor bikes to bicycles. And still thousands more came on foot.

By mid-morning, Rt. 17B was an unbroken ribbon of vehicles and humanity from near Monticello to White Lake and the Aquarian Festival.

Progress on this normally 50 miles-per-hour highway was measured in inches per hour. The road's shoulders were choked with cars parked by drivers who had decided walking would be faster. Hundreds of cars, hoods raised, steamed with overheated engines.

Idling motors guzzled fuel, but service stations along the road had run out of gas. Stores had long lines of young customers seeking provisions from dwindling shelves. At some places, milk reportedly was selling for a dollar a quart. A loaf of bread sold for the same price. Chances of fresh provisions being brought in via road were nil.

Cars not overheated or abandoned inched nearer to the festival with no hope of coming within sight or sound of it.

Some of those walking limped on blistered feet and many young people walking barefoot trod the hot asphalt gingerly, their backs bent by bedrolls and other belongings needed for the long weekend. Others slept on the grass along the highway and on tops of cars.

Every open field was dotted with cars and tents and at times, just blankets, like homesteaders claiming land they intended to make their homes.

But through it all a festive air prevailed, as if it were all a game of the young, and the frustrated and inconvenienced did not belong.

Residents along Rt. 17B stood on their lawns, sometimes reinforced by members of their family, to make sure tents were not pitched. Others assisted thirsty hikers with jugs of water.

Some residents felt completely cut off **from the outside world by the sea of young people and vehicles.**

One worried mother of three voiced her fears. "Who knows what they will do?" she said, as she watched the stream of humanity sweep past her home.

"We may not have enough food to last the weekend." Her husband had stayed home from work to be near his family.

Eldred, 15 miles from the site, had run out of bread by early afternoon. A truckload of bread ordered by a local supermarket sold out in the parking lot within five minutes of arriving at the store. A gas station attendant there estimated his fuel supply would last another half hour.

And they kept coming.

Photo by John De Lorenzo

Photo courtesy Cornelius Alexy

Aerial view of campground beside Filippini's Pond.

Meanwhile, in town there were thousands of kids milling around in search of food. Richard Cutler of Silicon Valley, California, remembers, "We hadn't eaten anything since lunch the day before. We joined up with this guy, Tommy, who knew the area, and he told us of a Jewish summer camp that wasn't too far away. We waded around the edge of a lake to get to there and were met by a suspicious camp director. He offered us a kosher meal if we would eat outside the camp infirmary away from the children."

Photo by Gary Geyer

Standing in line to get a peanut butter and jelly sandwich at Vassmer's General Store.

Photo by Gary Geyer

White Lake's sudden population explosion.

Photo by Gary Geyer

Making their way between the festival and town.

Friends and food. Looking for both.

Photo by Gary Geyer

Photo by Jim and Linda Breslin

Near the stage with the campground in the distance.

Photo by Jim and Linda Breslin

A view of the stage.

When Harriette Schwartz and her friend, Alan, arrived in White Lake, she recalls, "The memory of all these local residents lining the road and looking at us as if we were from Mars is forever emblazoned in my brain."

Photo by Harriette Schwartz

Harriette Schwartz on the way to Woodstock.

Photo by Harriette Schwartz

Alan, a friend of Harriette Schwartz, looks at the Woodstock concert program.

Photo by Derek Redmond and Paul Campbell

The sight of ambulances increased as did medical emergencies.

Photo by David Marks. (3rd Ear Music/Hidden Years Music Archives 1969-2009)

An exodus in mud and garbage.

As the day passed, medical emergencies were arising, and the organizers sent for doctors and nurses willing to help. Mary Sanderson, a 40-year-old nurse from Middletown, New York, recalls boarding a helicopter at dawn on Saturday and soaring toward Bethel in a battering hailstorm. Just before they arrived, sunshine shot through a hole in the clouds, and it looked like a scene from a biblical epic. "Being in a helicopter and seeing the sun's rays shining down on 500,000 people…it looked like the multitudes," Sanderson remembers. "You just can't picture that. You can't imagine how all those people looked in that sun."

The morning before Sanderson's arrival, sodden sleeping bags were churned with debris and discarded clothing. Standing rainwater was steaming skyward, blanketing thousands of sleeping kids with an eerie fog. Gery Krewson of Tunkhannock, Pennsylvania, watched as a tractor came rumbling over the hill as it plowed through heaps of soaked garbage and sleeping bags. It was towing a tank trailer hauling away sewage. Under that pile slept Raymond Mizak, a 17-year-old from South Jersey.

Christopher Cole recalls, "We noticed the tractor moving. It ran over what appeared to be a mound of mud, but a human arm flopped out. It was a kid in a mummy sleeping bag. I ran to the trailers and screamed for help," but by the time it arrived, Mizak was dead.

"We popped up the hospital tent called 'Big Pig,'" recalls Wavy Gravy. Jahanara remembers they were flying in medical teams to help with the influx of heat exhaustion and overdoses.

"Nobody knew what to do," Jahanara says. "With everything running smoothly at the kitchen, I went over to the medical area, and just as I got there, help arrived. A seminal event was when Abbie Hoffman entered the tent. He took charge, shouting instructions, and everyone listened. I mean, nobody knew who he was, and those who knew of him knew that he wasn't ordinarily in a situation to be ordering doctors and nurses around, but they needed some kind of order and he was making sense. He shouted, 'OK, if you are a person with a medical certification go stand in this corner,' 'If you're from the Hog Farm, go stand in this corner.'"

The festival's medical director was Dr. William Abruzzi of Wappingers Falls, New York, and when Mary Sanderson arrived, he immediately put her in charge of the newly erected medical tent. Nurse Sanderson remembers a man selling his own brand of medicine. "All day long he yelled out, 'Mescaline! One dollar!'"

Still photo taken from 8mm film, courtesy Randy Sheets.

Medical Tent and National Guard evacuation helicopter.

For the rest of the festival, Jahanara worked in the medical area. "One of the beautiful things about Woodstock was that you learned how to respect each other. The doctors learned to respect the hippies and visa versa. Although it didn't start out that way, it quickly got to be where we appreciated each other. Even several of the artists came in; John Sebastian serenaded people for quite a long time."

"The medical tents were up by the stage and were for actual medical emergencies," says Hog Farmer Jean Nichols. "We did the freak-out tents, which were different. I helped by circulating through the crowd, looking for anyone having a hard time. The people we helped, helped us. As soon as they'd get it back together, we'd put them in charge of the next person and give them the responsibility. That worked out really well. I do believe much of what the kids were experiencing was a perception resulting from the announcements. We knew that whenever warnings went out against the brown acid or whatever—there may have been three different kinds with only one being bad, but people wouldn't realize that. All it would take was someone to say, 'Oh, my God, you took the brown acid?' and that would be it."

"Abbie and his crew were printing," recalls Jahanara. "I don't know where they got a printing machine, but they were putting out daily flyers to keep people informed about such things as where broken water lines were or where help was needed. That was really helpful. We were a city with a daily paper run by Abbie Hoffman."

Trudy Morgal remembers flyers being passed along; they were like a survival guide. "I don't think they really believed anyone needed them. You don't need to tell someone that they're gonna get sunburned, but people were acting responsibly to provide assistance during the 'disaster.' A disaster I'd take any day."

SU VIVIE SURVIVE SURVIV SURVIVE SURVIVE SURVIVE S

We come to Hip City, USA. We' now one of the largest cities in America (population 300,000 a growing all the time). We've got ... traffic death, 15 miscarriages and a lot of mud. This is a d aster area.

Where we go from here depends on all of us. The people who promoted this festival have been overwhelmed by their own creation. We can no longer remain passive consumer / we have to begin to fend for ourselves

ACCESS -- The highways leading to the festival site are now blocked. Cars are being bturned back in an effort to clear highway 17B. The best thing you can do is to stay until the roads are cleared. If you decide to split and get stuck a team of repairmen is cruising the area and will free your car. n't leave your vehicle.

SANITATION -- Please stay off the roads. Garbage trucks need clear rights-of-way to pick up trash. Either burn your trash or dump it IN BAGS along the road (look r the stands with green bags hanging from them.) You MUST clean your area to avoid a severe health hazard.

MEDICAL -- There are two majo medical stations. Minor stuff (cuts, bruises) can be taken care of at the SOUTH STATION near the Hog Farm, serious injuries will be trea ed at the health trailer at the MAIN INTERSECTION, and drug freakouts will be tended by the Hog Farm (red armband) people at the SOUTH AMPGROUND.

A planeload of doctors are eing airlifted from New York City, and a fleet of helicopters is bei g gathered to drop medical supplies.

Any trained medical personn should report to the above medical centers.

Do not take any light blue lat acid and understand that taking strong dope at this time may ake you a drag in a survival situation.

Don't run naked in the hot un for any period of time. Water blisters are painful.

WATER -- Water is scarce. Share and conserve all water. Do not drink water unless it is crystal-clear. Check with festival and Hog Farm people before using any opera ing mains. New mains are being readied. We will announce their locati ns when they are made available. Blac k and white pipes are water pipes, on't use for walking or bridges. They break easily.

The lake is now a main sour e of water. Swimming will ruin the purification system -- think wic before taking a dip.

FOOD -- You should not be pig ish about your food and water. As with medicine, festival peopl have promised that food will be airlifted into the area. The og Farm will continue to serve meals in the SOUTH AREA.

VOLUNTEERS -- Go to info. st d a main intersection

GENERAL HINTS - The thing t do is survive and share. Organize your own camping area so tha everyone makes it through uncomfortable times ahead. Figure out what ou must do and the best ways to get it done.

PEOPLE WHO CANHELP DISTRIBU E THIS LEAFLET SHOULD COME TO THE MOVEMENT CITY AREA IN TE SOUTH CAMPG OUND.

READ AND PAS ON

One of Abbie Hoffman's Survival Guide flyers.

8 Saturday, August 16, 1969 THE TIMES HERALD RECORD

Blow-by-blow account

News breaks fast and hard at Aquarian fest

Throughout the day, Times Herald-Record reporters on the festival site and in Monticello filed hasty advisories to the main office in Middletown. Here are their reports, carried over a direct teletype line from the Town of Bethel festival site, through Monticello, to Middletown.

Fred Germain--Basic picture at 1 p.m. Near disaster in many respects. Water shortage said critical. Attendance now being estimated at 200 thousand. Traffic has become terrible...

• • •

This is Gil Weisinger at 1:10: Hospital picture still bleak. But A. F. Cacchillo, administrator of the community hospital with branches in Monticello and Liberty, said emergency measures have been taken to ensure the best medical facilities available.

Additional regular nurses have been placed on round-the-clock duty, all doctors in the county have been alerted, and auxiliary police have been stationed at the emergency rooms round-the-clock for the next three days.

He denied earlier reports that the hospitals were overcrowded, but agreed that he would be unable to handle an emergency situation of the 200,000 people reported at the site. He referred to the Middletown hospital and said it could always be used in an emergency.

• • •

This Gil with some more bad news. Just called civil defense office, and Asst. County Director, Mrs. Emily Rosch, says her office is not equipped to handle the emergency and she, at this point, does not intend to do anything about the siuation. More to come after I check with sheriff and social services commissioner...

• • •

This Gil again at 1:30... Just checked with sheriff's department. They say they are not preparing for any emergency at this time and are only handling traffic problems. They are diverting all traffic on Rt. 17 (The Quickway) past Monticello to Liberty for a round-about access to site.

Robert Travis, social services commissioner is unavailable for comments on emergency measures, but after speaking with civil defense and sheriff's departments, I doubt if he is taking any additional precautions.

• • •

White Lake--All original plans by Woodstock Ventures to sell tickets on the site have been scrapped. The turnstile system was not set up. All those who arrived ticketless had no one to answer to and were admitted free--thousands of them.

• • •

Germain at 1:35: Mayor Lindsay is expected in Monticello at 3 if he can get from new airport to Monticello in time to open campaign office.

• • •

This Gil in Monticello (to White Lake staff)--What the heck happened to the supposed medical facilities at the festival?

Scores of people dressed in hippie-type garb are milling about the streets of Monticello, many with sleeping gear strapped to their backs. Luncheonettes are doing a "land-office" business, and festival tickets, once in great demand and extremely scarce during the last hours before the fest; are not being peddled on the streets for anything the holders can get.

Many people with tickets are approaching sales outlets for refunds, but are being told to refund their tickets through the fest promoters direct. Some people are even trying to give tickets away and those offered the freebies are just shaking their heads in a negative response.

• • •

Late announcement... Monticello Village Manager Thomas Belmont and Village Fire Chief William Lane have asked all paid firemen and all volunteers to report for duty on a standby basis.

• • •

White Lake to Gil and Middletown from Expo. Re: Hospital.

Woodstock promoters were operating a 20-bed hospital on the site but area hospitals reported admissions for broken toes and fingers and unfavorable drug experiences. Nearby Liberty and Monticello hospitals reported they were filled to capacity. There has been some ambulance service in the area but I don't know details yet...

• • •

This Gil... Promoters had originally pledged a 60-bed hospital at the site, four doctors, and about six registered nurses. This info obtained from the Rev. Donald Ganoung, assistant chief security, and Mel Lawrence, festival director.

• • •

White Lake advisory at 3:45 p.m.--Fifteen minutes remain before the scheduled start of the Aquarian Exposition. Tens of thousands are seated in the amphitheater. A few squawks from the loudspeaker system hint that all systems are go. Rumors are rife that some of the contemporary superstars were victims of the gigantic traffic jam.

• • •

4:15 p.m.--Not a murmur from the stage as yet. TH-R trailer not within sight but within sound of earlier squawks from the loudspeaker system. If delay continues--coupled with all the logistical difficulties faced by the paying and unpaying audience, the crowd could turn very unhappy (to say the least).

• • •

This Gil in Monticello with advisory at 4:20 p.m. on drug arrests... Just spoke to Thompson Town magistrate Joseph Wasser. He is setting $1,000 bail for possession of drugs and $20,000 for sale. He has had 15 brought before him since last night--four for sale and 11 for possession.

Was tied up and unable to give more info. But am checking jail which must be filled to capacity (or more) by now.

Line has been constantly busy at the jail but am still trying. Other judges must be having the same brisk business and will check with them as soon as possible.

• • •

4:30--Not a sound from the stage yet.

Advisory from Middletown to White Lake... Federal Aviation Agency has prohibited planes from flying less than 2,500 feet over festival site. Hinders our try for aerial art but are trying to get it anyway by unconvential use of a telephoto lens.

• • •

This Gil at 4:35--Mayor Lindsay has just cancelled his Monticello appearance. Festival jam-up kept him at Sullivan airport, seven miles away from Monticello.

• • •

URGENT--Woodstock Pres. John Roberts has just begun urging people on way to festival to turn back... more as we get it.

• • •

Monticello to Middletown: Lindsay has left airport for Grossinger's via back roads.

• • •

This White Lake at 4:59--Roar of applause goes up following landing of six copters. Indications are that performers are aboard.

• • •

URGENT: Sheriff's department has just closed off Exit 104, which serves festival and Monticello Raceway. Festival people being sent to Exit 101, raceway fans to 102.

• • •

Gil here at 5:05... Civil Defense Asst. Director Emily Rosch "went home" and the C. D. office in the county courthouse in Monticello is being manned by Jeff Blumenfeld, who is operating citizens band radios between the festival site and Monticello. Civil Defense has apparently thrown its hands up over the situation and the office has been taken over by conscientious citizens.

Blumenfeld and others are providing traffic information via CB radios between Monticello and the site.

• • •

White Lake to news desk: At 5:07 p.m., singer Richie Havens laid apprehensions to rest and kicked off the three-day rock festival and hour and seven minutes late.

A long line of cars and humanity inch their way toward White Lake and the Aquarian Festival late Friday morning. Despite waiting in line for hours, thousands of cars and ticket holders did not get within sight of the afternoon concert. *TH-Record photo by Manny Fuchs*

Photo by Cornelius Alexy

Mud and trash begin to transform the field.

The attendance was estimated at 250,000 that morning, making it the largest audience in history.

Photo by John De Lorenzo

Groovin'.

The crowd.

Photo by Derek Redmond and Paul Campbell

Promoters knew early on that it was crucial to crowd control for the music to be endless, especially after dark. Music was scheduled to start at 7 p.m. on Saturday and continue until midnight, but the promoters changed their strategy after Friday night's crowd. They needed more music and decided that the acts should start later and play until dawn. Saturday's bill included loud, hard rock and roll: The Who, Jefferson Airplane, Janis Joplin, Creedence Clearwater Revival, the Grateful Dead, Canned Heat, Mountain, and Santana. A concern was that the crowd could get wilder as the music got louder, but a greater worry was that bored fans could do damage if they weren't entertained. Michael Lang and the other organizers pleaded with Saturday's acts to play twice as long as scheduled, and most were willing. The attendance was estimated at 250,000 that morning, making it the largest audience in history.

Still photo taken from 8mm film, courtesy Randy Sheets.

The drone of helicopters was a constant reminder of the need for life support.

Photo by Derek Redmond and Paul Campbell

Photo by Derek Redmond and Paul Campbell

One of the beautiful things about Woodstock was that you learned how to respect each other.

Photo by Derek Redmond and Paul Campbell

Photo by Stephen Teso

Stephen Teso watched as performer after performer was flown in.

© Elliott Landy/Landyvision.com

Janis Joplin was one of many top name artists in the performer's pavilion.

Morgal remembers seeing the helicopter bring in Janis Joplin. "She came early and just hung out. You could see it was her. We were really excited."

Twelve-year-old Chuck Early of Huntington Beach, California, remembers that his mom was sitting with a group of people playing guitar and just having fun. "She called me over to hug some lady, but I was a little embarrassed; she wasn't wearing a shirt. Mom said it was ok, so I did. Much to my surprise, I had her muddy breast prints on my t-shirt, and all I knew was that I didn't like the way it looked. I went straight to the first mud puddle I could find to get dirtier and cover it up. I really wasn't much into girls yet, so that's why I reacted the way I did. I wish I knew what I had. Janis Joplin's boobs on my chest!"

Photo by Jim and Linda Breslin

Sleeping and sitting always required the cooperation of those around you.

Harriette Schwartz says, like many others, she kept working her way up to the front. Eventually she was about 50 feet from the stage, almost dead center. "Obviously, the closer we got, the more crowded it became," she says. "Thus, sleeping and sitting always involved the cooperation of those around you. You may have slept with your head on someone's knees, and yet another person's head on yours. If nothing else, it was a very interesting way get to know your neighbors."

Tom Sperry, 20, of Le Roy, New York, found a spot about 100 yards away, directly in front of the stage. The rain lifted, but now it was hot and humid, and they were exhausted after their long walk but glad to finally be there. The music started with an unknown group named Quill, followed by more acts and more rain.

Schwartz watched as Army helicopters flew over the crowd in the rain; they tossed out oranges to the people below as everyone reached to catch. "Of course," she says, "to also avoid a concussion!"

"The skies just opened up," remembers Tommy Hayes. "We got soaked, stuck in the middle of this mass of people while it poured. You couldn't get anywhere; there was no place to go. I could see the stage, but from a distance, and it was almost impossible to get any closer. There were too many people, and the mud was slippery. I noticed a bunch of people having fun with slides made out of mud. I watched a while, as people would run, jump, and slide as far as they could. Now when I see that clip in the movie, I cringe a little, but back then it was all fun stuff."

"We danced in the rain and were actually surprised when it stopped, even if it was just for a little while," says Chuck Early. "I remember a girl (named Delilah, I think). She was wearing a set of fairy wings and wore flowers in her hair like a crown. We were drinking raindrops as they fell on our tongues. Someone was playing 'Locomotion,' and we started a big dancing chain that went on for hundreds of people."

The rain turned the hillside to mud, and this discomfort provoked a communal spirit of concern and togetherness among the crowd. State authorities were calling the festival a "disaster area," but Woodstock was preparing to soar toward a euphoric peak.

Photo by Harriette Schwartz

The crowd sitting around Harriette Schwartz and her friend, Alan.

Photo by Jean Nichols

Watching comfortably on the stage after the rain lifted.

Photo courtesy Peter J. Carrigan, www.vintagerockandrollphotos.com

We are one.

The afternoon featured a series of spectacular performances by Santana, Mountain, and Canned Heat. Caleb Rossiter remembers the first cross-cultural moment for the white Woodstock Nation came with guitarist Carlos Santana. He had created his band of Chicanos to express rock and roll in Latin rhythms.

"Like most of the crowd, I had never listened to Latin music and knew nothing of its tradition as a companion to revolution," says Rossiter. "Earlier generations may have had their epiphany about the breadth of the world in a classroom or on a trip with their parents, but mine was Santana's celebration of a culture so near, yet so far." Santana's nine-minute, 39-second instrumental, 'Soul Sacrifice,' solidified Woodstock as a bona fide musical 'happening.'"

Dancing in the sun.

Photo by Derek Redmond and Paul Campbell

Carlos Santana credits his famous facial contortions on stage to the taking of hallucinogens prior to performing. His guitar was like a serpent in his hands, which took a great deal of concentration to tame.

Photo by David Marks (3rd Ear Music/Hidden Years Music Archives 1969-2009)

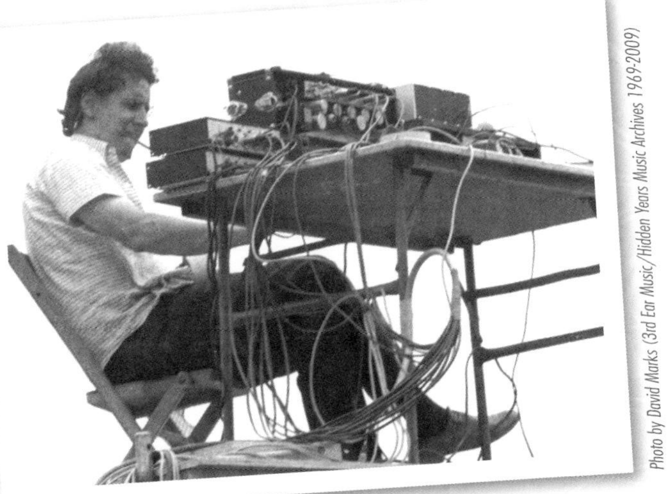

Photo by David Marks (3rd Ear Music/Hidden Years Music Archives 1969-2009)

Bill Hanley, "The Father of Festival Sound." His talents brought the music of Woodstock to the ears of a half million.

Photo by David Marks (3rd Ear Music/Hidden Years Music Archives 1969-2009)

Getting the sound just right—Hanley put his sound mixer in the crowd, in front of the stage, something seen at every modern concert since. Sound comes of age at Woodstock.

"I remember that it was Jimi Hendrix's agent who got us on the show," says Leslie West of Mountain. "We had the same agent, and if they wanted Hendrix, they had to take us. We were out at the Fillmore West and Winterland, and we heard about what was going on back east, and knew we were going. When we arrived in New York we had to rent our own helicopter. There was no way we were getting upstate with the freeway closed and all that, so I didn't know what to make of it. We were in the helicopter and flew over, I looked down, and I almost fell out of the helicopter when I saw all those people. I said, 'Jesus Christ.' You know, it was like all of a sudden in the middle of nowhere you saw a city. It was something else."

Caleb Rossiter says, "Leslie West was massive, and his guitar looked like a toy in his hands." John De Lorenzo recalls, "Mountain blew us away. By far, they were the most memorable. West's guitar playing and voice astonished us; we'd never heard of them before. I think they opened with 'Blood of the Sun' but 'Dreams of Milk and Honey' was on their play list and became forever etched in our minds."

Photo by David Marks (3rd Ear Music/Hidden Years Music Archives 1969-2009)

Bill Hanley designed, built, and operated the sound system. His innovations made Woodstock famous for not only the mud and music, but for evolving sound engineering. Hanley also did sound for the Beatles' second U.S. tour.

© Elliott Landy/Landyvision.com

Tommy "Purple" Hayes, 16, in striped pants climbing the sound tower.

"I don't remember [the performance]," West says with a laugh. "I was really nervous. I do know that when I did my guitar solo, I had my four stacks hooked up and Felix's stacks hooked up. I think I had eight stacks of amps, so it sounded pretty loud. I was wondering how those people in the back were going to hear...how are they going to hear me? But I guess they did."

Tommy Hayes wanted a good seat for Canned Heat. He tried to get down to the stage, but that didn't happen, so he decided to climb the tower. "A lot of guys were doing it," he says. "When I started climbing, there were people above me. I remember this one guy had to pee—and proceeded to do so, on everyone below. I thought to myself, 'Oh God, this is horrible.' I watched as this was happening and tried to keep out of the way. I guess he had to be really messed up to do something like that. It was crazy! I continued my climb and got myself pretty much up there, perched on a crossbar, and got to see Canned Heat perfectly."

Hailed as blues innovators, Canned Heat was now spreading the gospel worldwide with its newest album, "Livin' the Blues," which brought forth "Goin' Up the Country," a song that defined Woodstock and made Canned Heat a household name.

Fito de la Parra [in an interview with *Goldmine Magazine's* Peter Lindblad] recalls, "One of the funny things was, I didn't want to go. I was really exhausted. I didn't know how important it was going to be; to me, it was just another gig. That night Skip Taylor [our manager] got a key to my room, and if he hadn't been there I wouldn't have gotten out of bed. He turned on the TV and said, 'Look at this! There are all these people out there. This is going to be a great gig. Come on, let's go!'"

Photo by Harriette Schwartz

Harriette Schwartz's and Alan's view of Canned Heat.

The thought of performing in his state of mind was so repellant that de la Parra actually quit. "I said, 'F___ you, I'm quitting. I hate this shit.' Skip basically pulled me out of bed—he was bigger than me anyway. He dressed me up and off we went. We made it to the festival by 'copter a few hours later. 'My God!' I said, 'Look at these people.' And that's when I realized, 'I'm glad Skip got me up.'"

Speaking with Stu Fox, de la Parra says that though the band was tense, its energy was electric, and the group's show is often cited as one of the highlights of the event. "I think we got the best ovation of the festival," says de la Parra.

"They were just booking," says Trudy Morgal. "They had their engine crankin' and the crowd in a frenzy. It was driving music and I really enjoyed them. It was all that energy they were putting off. It was something."

© Elliott Landy/Landyvision.com

A fan shares the love with Canned Heat's Bob "the Bear" Hite.

Photo courtesy Peter J. Corrigan, www.vintagerockandrollphotos.com

Alan Wilson (Canned Heat) delivering the blues.

Between acts there were long waits as equipment was dismantled and the next group set up. Tommy Hayes remembers that after two days they really needed to clean up, and since there was time, they decided to make their way to Filippini's Pond.

"Everyone was washing and bathing, and as we got closer we could see a lot people skinny-dipping. Here was another new experience!" Hayes recalls. "I peeled off my clothes and jumped right in. I frolicked in the water, nude, and it felt great—a freedom; a cleansing of the spirit. It was nice and all good-natured. Thinking about it now, the water probably wasn't as clean as we thought, but it was wet. We'd been rained on, sat through dust and humidity, baked by the sun, and muddied all over. The lake was something we all needed."

Hanging out by Forsythia Cove.

Photo by Gary Geyer

"Peace!" at Filippini's Pond.

Photo by Gary Geyer

Photo by Gary Geyer

Photo by Gary Geyer

Climbing to the wall.

Photo by Gary Geyer

Several in the lake.

As we got closer we could see a lot people skinny-dipping... I peeled off my clothes and jumped right in.

Photo by Gary Geyer

Cooling off at a small falls near Forsythia Cove.

Gary Geyer.

Photo by Gary Geyer

Skinny-dippers.

Photo by Gary Geyer

Fun and frolicking.

Photo by Gary Geyer

Howie Cohen.

Photo by Gary Geyer

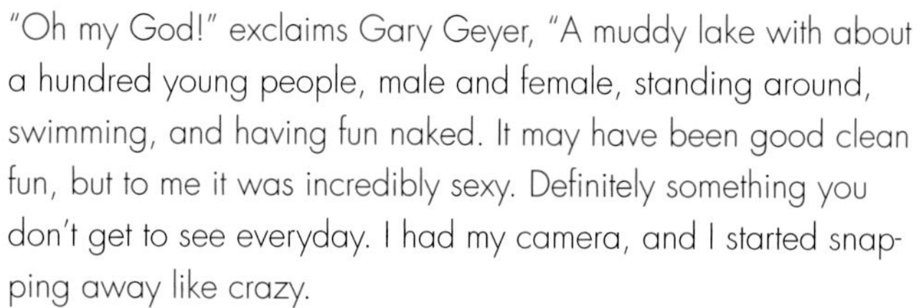

"Oh my God!" exclaims Gary Geyer, "A muddy lake with about a hundred young people, male and female, standing around, swimming, and having fun naked. It may have been good clean fun, but to me it was incredibly sexy. Definitely something you don't get to see everyday. I had my camera, and I started snapping away like crazy.

"After watching for about 10 minutes, we thought, 'Why not?' and joined everyone else. Nobody knew us and I have to say, we really got into it and surprised ourselves. There is something about public nudity that obviously brings out the best in people."

Ninety-year-old Ben Leon ran a boat rental business on Filippini's Pond, popularly known as "Leon's Lake." Leon wasn't renting boats that weekend, but he kept watch from a porch on the hill-side overlooking the largest of Woodstock's skinny-dipping spots.

"He sat on the veranda, the old fool, with a giant pair of binoculars, and you could hear him 50 feel away: 'Heee-heee-heee. Haw-haww-haww,'" then-Bethel historian Bert Feldman remarks. Sad to say, 10 days after the festival, Leon dropped dead. "I talked to the undertaker," Feldman says, "and he told me he couldn't wipe the smile off the guy's face. That's the way to go, I guess."

Photo by Gary Geyer

Photo by Gary Geyer

Boating on Filippini's Pond.

Modesty abandoned.

Photo by Gary Geyer

Photo by Gary Geyer

Showering the "Woodstock" way.

Photo by Gary Geyer

Heading to the water.

Breaks in music didn't mean breaks in offerings from the stage. Tom Law taught yoga over by the Hog Farm camp, and once between acts, Lisa recalls, "I looked out and saw people sitting up and doing deep breathing with their hands in a mudra pose. It was beautiful."

Nick Ercoline fondly remembers the two beautiful blonde girls walking toward him and Bobbi Kelly, wearing nothing but kitchen curtains. "They were sheer kitchen curtains," Kelly interjects." And I got to tell you, there was no back fat back in those days. We worked our way in as far as we could get, and found our spot on the east side of the top plateau."

"I think the amazing shot," says Ercoline, "was just the sea of heads. That's all you saw. And the lighting was basically red and yellow, which gave an orange glow; it's something I'll never forget."

"I was sitting on the blanket just over the crest of the hill," Bobbi says. "You couldn't see the stage, but you could hear [the music]. Among that sound you could hear other people playing their guitars and other instruments, people laughing, children playing, the chatter, the overall patter. Now it was night, and to look out from where I sat, you could see hundreds of different parties going on. It was humid, heavy, hot, wet, soggy-smelling, swampy- smelling, puke-smelling, campfire-smelling, pot-smelling, food cooking, body odor, combined with the din of thousands of voices, and sounds from everywhere; it assaulted your senses. It was sensory overload, and it was the best place in the world at that time. It really was."

After dark, Creedence Clearwater Revival ripped through a set that had the crowd dancing in the mud. "They were the one performance I clearly remember," recalls Sha Na Na's Jocko Marcellino. "I remember turning back and seeing all these campfires as Creedence was rockin' out on 'Born on the Bayou.'"

During a steady drizzle, Grateful Dead took the stage. U.S. Army's C. Duane Noto, 20, stationed at Fort Monmouth, New Jersey, remembers, "My friend and I were huge Grateful Dead fans, before 'deadhead' was even a word. We were telling everyone around us to get ready for the best band at the show and promised that the whole field would be dancing. Well, to the contrary, the Dead had one of their worst shows ever."

"It was intimidating for us seeing 400,000 people out there, and the stage was collapsing," says Mickey Hart. "Jerry [Garcia] and Bob [Weir] were getting shocked at the microphones. There were too many people on the stage, and we were hearing screams that it was sinking. It just wasn't our day."

Ira Stone, Bert Sommer's guitar player, remembers, "It was the first time I saw the Dead. After their set, Jerry Garcia was sitting on a stone wall near the backstage tent area, smiling that big Cheshire cat smile. I said, 'Jerry, you guys were great!' He just stared, smiled, and said, 'F___ you.' That was a little strange, but he wasn't being mean or anything."

By this time, Trudy Morgal needed the bathroom. She recalls that "the porta-potties were muddy, I mean muddy! Brown tracked in and brown tracked out. It smelled like shit, and it looked like shit, and I'm trippin'. I had this little light, white on one side, flashing red on the other, but by this time the white light had burnt out. So here I am in this stall with my light flashing red, red, red and I see this brown all over. Now I'm hearing, 'If anyone has any extra blankets, please bring them to the emergency tent,' 'Joe so-and-so, please come get your insulin.' It was like, 'Oh, my God! What's going on?' I'm sitting in this shit hole with a red light going on and off, and all I had to eat today was peaches. I felt like shit and everything was in motion. Finally, I turned off the light and it helped," and when her world stopped spinning, she made her way back to the bus.

Photo courtesy Goldmine Magazine

Grateful Dead.

Following the Grateful Dead, Janis Joplin graced the stage with a riveting set that included "Try," "Ball and Chain," and "Piece of My Heart."

It was Sly and the Family Stone that soon rocketed the music into the stratosphere. "Everybody was just rockin' and rollin' and going crazy during Sly's performance" says Trudy Morgal. "I was standing on a couple of milk crates to see up over the crowd. It was a great view, and I can't believe I didn't fall off. That was one of the high points for me because, at that time, there weren't a lot of funk bands out. There was definitely more white music going on, and being a drummer…when Sly came out I thought, 'This is the deal, man.'"

[Freddie:] Feeling's gettin' stronger
[Larry:] Music's gettin' longer, too
[Rose:] Music is flashin' me
[Sly:] I wanna. I want to take you higher
Baby, baby, baby, light my fire
[All:] Boom shaka-laka-laka,
boom shaka-laka-laka
—Sly and the Family Stone

Greg Henry remembers, "During 'I Want to Take You Higher,' every single person was on their feet, clapping and stomping. I remember standing still; I could feel the ground beneath me rumble. I told my friend to try it, and we just stood there with these huge smiles on our faces. It was amazing. Sly had everyone dancing and some with torches made by tying shirts on sticks and setting them afire."

Photo by Don Aters

Janis Joplin.

Everybody was just rockin' and rollin' and going crazy.

Photo by Derek Redmond and Paul Campbell

Janis Joplin.

Photo by Derek Redmond and Paul Campbell

The Who. Daltrey with his arms out in his Messiah-like stance and Townshend assaults his guitar with his trademark "windmill."

C. Duane Noto remembers that he and his barracks mate decided to go for a day trip. They just heard about Woodstock and decided to see how close they could get. Not knowing the lineup, they were amazed when The Who took the stage. They had just listened to "Tommy" for the very first time a few hours before. Now they were watching the English rockers perform the theme song "See Me, Feel Me" live.

The fringe-shirted Roger Daltrey sang, "Listening to you, I get the music…gazing at you, I get the heat…" while Head Yippie Abbie Hoffman was sitting on the stage with Michael Lang. Hoffman had been working the medical tent, gobbling tabs of acid to stay awake, and had become increasingly obsessed with publicizing the case of John Sinclair, a Michigan teen-ager busted for the possession of two marijuana cigarettes.

He jumped up, grabbed the mike, and started spewing out words about Sinclair, who had received a 10-year jail sentence. The Who's lead guitarist, Pete Townshend, didn't recognize Hoffman and figured he was just another whacked-out festival-goer rushing the stage, so he bonked Abbie on the head with his guitar. Hoffman wandered away.

"Abbie was just being Abbie," says Artie Kornfeld. "He was out of his head at Woodstock. He didn't have contact with reality."

The Who continued the intensity, and the first light of morning appeared in the sky as they rocked out another Woodstock anthem.

Photo by Derek Redmond and Paul Campbell

The Who ends with a destructive blow to Townshend's guitar.

People try to put us d-down
(talkin' 'bout my generation)
Just because we get around
(talkin' 'bout my generation)
Things they do look awful c-c-cold
(talkin' 'bout my generation)
I hope I die before I get old
(talkin' 'bout my generation)
—Pete Townshend

Linda Breslin remembers, "For three days it was music…sleep…music…sleep…and more music. We listened, lived, and slept in the field. You'd fall asleep rolling on the neighbor next to you, or behind you, and that was fine."

As the sun crested Sunday, Grace Slick's voice wafted out of the festival bowl to a pasture above:

"One pill makes you larger, and one pill makes you small…."

The psychedelic rumblings of Jefferson Airplane brought the day's music marathon to a furious conclusion.

For three days it was music…sleep…music…sleep…and more music.

Photo by Derek Redmond and Paul Campbell

Jefferson Airplane's Paul Kantner, Grace Slick, and Marty Balin.

Chapter 4

"I'M A FARMER..."—MAX YASGUR TO THE WOODSTOCK CROWD

DAY THREE – SUNDAY, AUG. 17, 1969

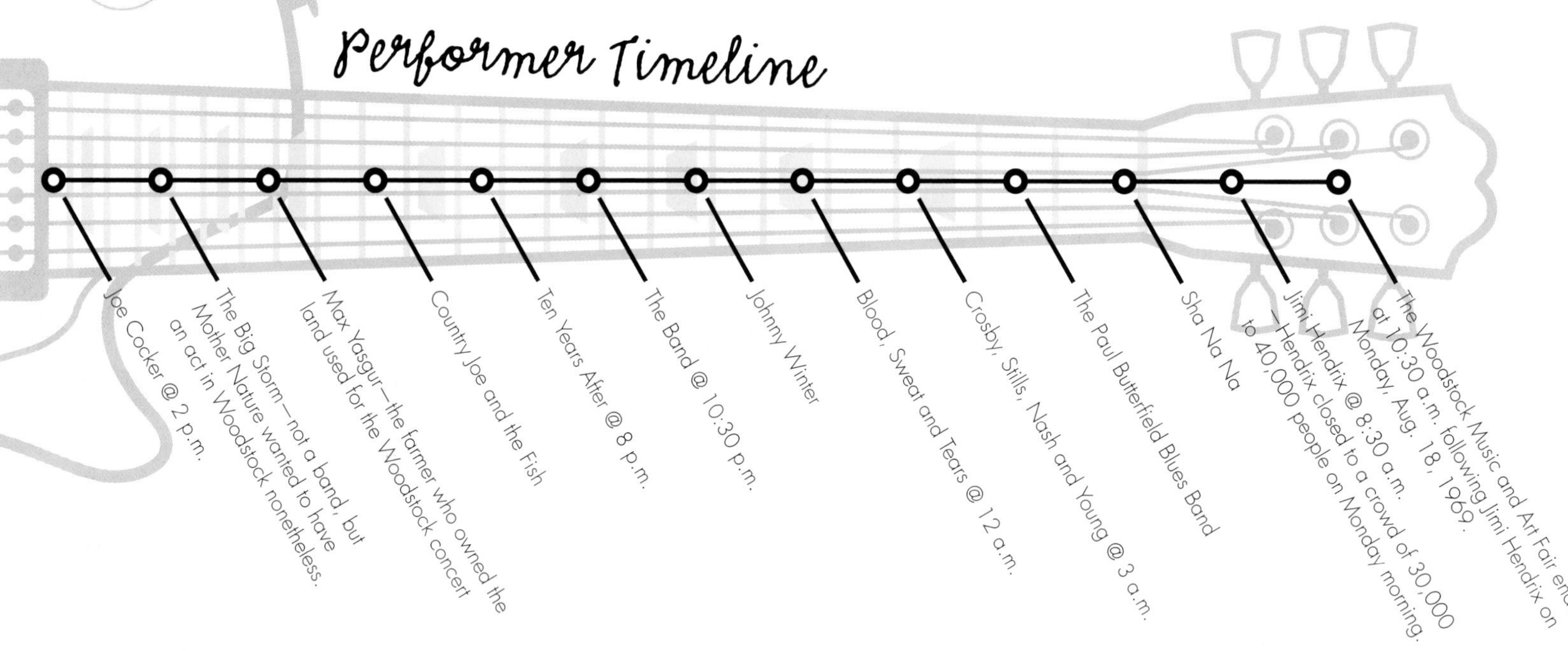

The Times Herald
RECORD

Weather: Warm | Middletown, N.Y. 10940 | Monday morning, August 18, 1969 | 10 Cents

2 dead as 450,000 begin fest exodus

Other stories, photos, Pages 2-9

By A. N. ROMM
Editor

WHITE LAKE

Torrential rain at mid-afternoon Sunday triggered an early exodus of thousands from the music-and-drug haven known as the Aquarian Exposition.

Even as problem-plagued festival officials and weary police braced for a reverse traffic jam with an undisclosed plan for a one-way network out of the area, thousands of the 450,000 sardined into this 600-acre Sodom-Disneyland combination are expected to camp a week or two more on premises.

Aquarian promoters, who admittedly "took a bath" for hundreds of thousands of dollars, consider themselves morally as well as legally responsible for maintaining food, water, and sanitation services for the uninvited residue.

Rep. Martin B. McKneally of Newburgh R-27, Sunday called the festival a "disgraceful act." He censured all public and private individuals who brought the hundreds of thousands into the area "without proper preparation."

The monumental problems posed by an underprepared site and an influx four times greater than planned may mark the death of music festivals of this sort.

"I don't see how anyone can afford to do this again," one Aquarian staff aide forecast Sunday.

For lack of turnstiles and fencing, two out of three festival-goers got in free. One in three had paid in advance.

Medical and drug-related problems continued to dominate the festival scene.

A second death Sunday at Horton Memorial Hospital was attributed to an overdose of drugs. An unidentified youth had been rushed from the site. The first death was Saturday when Raymond R. Mizsak, 17, of Trenton, was run over by a tractor as he lay in a sleeping bag in a muddy field.

Two other youths were reported in critical condition at Horton from drug overdoses. A third was operated on for a fractured skull.

First aid and medical squads on the festival site treated at least 3,000 during the weekend. Saturday 12

Continued on Page 3

Volunteers carry Henry Weitzman, 74, of Flushing, L. I., after he accidentally set himself afire Sunday at the Aquarian Exposition. Leaking fuel from a container spilled on his shoes and socks, igniting them. He was in fair condition in Monticello Community General Hospital.
--TH-Record photo by Mike Lee

6 Monday, August 18, 1969 THE TIMES HERALD RECORD

Surrealistic sights compete with rock singers

By JOE SHEA

WHITE LAKE

A naked youth, his muscular body glistening with sweat, danced suggestively around a fire ringed by scores of strangely-garbed hippies beating out demonic, pulsating sounds on bongo drums, tin cans and anything else available.

Deep in the front of the massive amphitheatre, other youths passed "Joints" (marijuana cigarettes) as Janis Joplin belted out what one girl called "the heaviest soul of all time.

In a makeshift lean-to perched among rocks on a hill overlooking the festival site, six Orange County youths shared a single can of sphagetti sauce for breakfast. They had just returned, weary but excited, from Saturday night's dusk till dawn concert featuring such rock names as Sly and the Family Stone, The Who, and Creedence Clearwater Revival.

It was a fantastic night. Blue, orange and white floodlights played across a crowd estimated at 400,000, and on the almost surrealistic stage their gods and goddesses flung out to them crescendo after crescendo of powerful sound.

From the fringes of the natural amphitheatre one could easly imagine a pillar of sound rising from the shining steel of instruments up to the dawn-breaking sky. When Sly and The Family Stone told the crowd "I want to get you higher, higher." Thousands of young people raised their hands in the famous two-fingered "high" sign.

When England's "The Who" took the stage, a massive roar climbed from the troats of the crowd and out over the mountains. A youth jumped to the stage and commandeered the microphone, telling the crowd that he thought the affair was meaningless as long as John Sinclair "rotted" in jail for possession of two marijuana cigarettes.

Peter Thompson, lead guitarist for the group, lifted his guitar and clubbed the youth into the pit in front of the stage. When a photographer with a movie camera moved in on the stage to film its lead singer, Thompson kicked the man in the pants, and he too fell headlong off the stage.

Janis Joplin throws herself body and soul into the soul music she is famed for...

Merchants praise hippies' behavior

By GIL WEISINGER

MONTICELLO

Despite a few scattered reports to the contrary, area merchants have praised the behavior of the estimated 400,000 Aquarian Exposition patrons.

From every section of Sullivan County, complimentary remarks pour in, most in the superlative such as "most polite, best behaved people I have ever met" and "they are the best mannered customers I have ever experienced."

At first the merchants were a little apprehensive about the strange-looking types, sporting beards, long hair, bizarre dress, and a language not frequently heard in the Catskills.

But during the emergency situation, people of all walks of life were thrown together and the hippies met the "straights" head on. Fears were dispelled as each became familiar with the other.

There has been no problem with shoplifting, something merchants are accustomed to with summer vacationers. In fact, one merchant reported, the trouble does not stem from the hippies, but from the "crew cut set."

Joe Rustic, who operates Rustic's restaurant in Monticello, said, "I sure have changed my opinion of these kids since I have had the opportunity to come in contact with them ... they are so polite."

Men called into service as auxiliary police have said they never expected anything like it. "If these hippies bump into you, they actually say excuse me," said one astounded officer. Despite the long lines of traffic, probably the worst jam ever experienced in the country, not one horn was leaned on, said a traffie control officer.

The festival patrons are composed of hippies, college students dressed like hippies, and the older generation. But the stabilizing factor, which keeps the behavior of all under control, is attributed to the "real hippies," many authorities say.

Their willingness to share their goods, their polite manners, and their general all around cheerfulness seems to be contagious. Authorities, expecting trouble even before any starts, are taken aback when their orders are met with a well-mannered response.

This in turn changes the attitude of the authorities and makes for good feelings in both camps, observers said.

Mrs. Minnie Schoen, a Liberty housewife, reported that she was "surprised" at the attitude of the long-haired types shopping in a local supermarket.

"They are quiet -- not like most of the vacationers -- and don't push their grocery carts into your back to get you out of the way," she said. What surprised her most, she added, was that they consistently said "Excuse me." One shopper dropped her bag of groceries, Mrs. Schoen said, and immediately a bunch of hippies came running over to help.

"This response would never come from the ordinary shopper I have seen," she said.

Sussex hospital receives gifts

SUSSEX, N.J.

Two gifts, one of $2,400 from Mr. and Mrs. Louis Markovits and another of $3,000 from Food City, operated by the Markovits and Menter families, have been received by the Alexander Linn Hospital, Sussex, N.J.

The announcement was made by Clifton E. Lawrence, chairman of the hospital's $300,000 building fund campaign. The combined subscription of $5,400 will build and equip a day room on the ground floor of the proposed wing to be added to the hospital's present building.

Photo by Kerby Smith

...while the dawn breaks over a mass of fans listening to the Jefferson Airplane.

Music is rallying call for the 'now' generation

By MARIAN and MARVIN FEMAN
Music Editors

Here are some thoughts that occurred during our 14-hour return trip from the Aquarian Exposition in White Lake to Middletown:

Music is the "open sesame" to this generation of Americans. It is the rallying call - as vital as speech. Music is the means to communicate, not only about music itself, but about its comments on love and the social forces shaping our lives - on the vision of a new idyllic tomorrow; a time of peace, tranquility and universal brotherhood - on the nature of self-fulfillment through whatever means or expressive idioms are available.

Music today contains a conglomeration of many styles, with many performers using one or more in combination. These diverse and compelling styles and forms have pervaded the American musical scene for more than 200 years.

Call it what you will, but these basic components are present in greater or lesser degree everywhere in today's music. Blues, both black and white, folk, gospel, jazz, western, country and hillbilly, plus the influences of India and other cultures - they are all present- giving us a wide spectrum of offerings that cater to every kind of musical appetite.

The musical scene is moving rapidly. Changes are swift, sometimes sudden and dramatic, but constantly traveling on. Stereotypes of the past have all but disappeared. It is no longer tenable to put rock and pop music down as inferior.

For many older Americans almost half a century of jazz may have mellowed its place in the current musical arena but it too is continuously exploring new directions. Rock has simply infused new excitements on the present scene. And when jazz and rock have come together - the result has not been a clash - but a new vitalization for both and a music with greater impact and appeal.

From a musical point of view we are optimistic about the future. The current generation of young Americans identify themselves with music and through music to each other. But in every generation, in every era of man's recorded history of civilization, music has played a vital role of sustenance and regeneration.

True it was then and true it is now. Today's music offers to those so inolined a choice of selecting his own musical delights from a widening assortment of varieties. What it all is basically stating is that current and popular tastes in music gives each individual an opportunity to do his own thing" and no passport is needed.

The overwhelming mass of humanity that sprawled below us as we swooped over the ridge is my strongest memory.

Sunday's lineup was again packed with rockers: The Band, Joe Cocker, Crosby, Stills & Nash, Ten Years After, Johnny Winter, and Jimi Hendrix. Attendance estimates kept rising, and the state police figure was 450,000, while others rounded it off to an even half-million.

By Sunday every portable toilet was filled to capacity, and the mud was at least six inches deep. Babette Brackett remembers, "My husband [Josh] said our situation was much like being in the Army. We were the officers, well prepared; most everyone else were enlisted men saved by the National Guard when they dropped care packages of food and water."

Port-o-san sewage truck near the overflowing facilities.

Still photo taken from 8mm film, courtesy Randy Sheets.

"We traveled from the Holiday Inn in Liberty to the festival site by means of the promoters' contracted heavy military-style chopper," remembers Donny York. "It was the first helicopter ride for us Sha Na Na guys. The background noise of a healthy engine accompanied our first sighting of it all. Holy gawd, it was like a scene from that *War and Peace* movie! Thousands and thousands of troops bivouacked down below, made more picturesque by occasional campfires. I thought the real question might be how they were doing for life support?"

Leo Lyons, bass player for Ten Years After, remembers that Woodstock was the group's fourth U.S. tour. "We'd played many festivals before Woodstock, and until we arrived, I didn't expect anything different from the others. That morning we took the red eye flight from St. Louis to New York City and intended to drive the rest of the way. The limo driver told us that things were crazy upstate and that traffic was backed up all the way to the festival. With some delay, we eventually did make it to the Holiday Inn.

"It was surreal. The hotel appeared to be a holding camp for festival musicians," says Lyons. "In the lobby and coffee shop, I remember seeing Jimi Hendrix, Janis Joplin, members of The Who, and many others I knew personally. The whole place was packed and helicopters were transporting bands from the hotel to the backstage area. I recall the green fields and farmhouses, but the overwhelming mass of humanity that sprawled below us as we swooped over the ridge is my strongest memory. The chopper deposited us close to the backstage area, and we walked around the enclosure, trying to take in the whole crazy scene. I could see this huge mass of people disappearing way up the hillside as far as the eye could see."

"Once off the big helicopter and past the ego rush of clearly being 'somebody,' people were eyeballing and shutter-bugging," says Donny York. "My impression was that a crew of hippie sorts had a reasonably confident grip on life support—imbibing and eliminating both possible enough—complete with an island or two of shade under tenting. The smells were of people's eats and smokes and sweat, and yes, patchouli oil." This was Sunday, the final scheduled day of the festival, and "no rain" was over 24 hours ago. "We actually believed someone's pronouncement that, around 9 p.m., we'd go on for about 25 minutes," says York. "It was a great hour for our three gold lame-costumed front guys to shimmer under the lights."

Lyons recalls, "I was talking to some of the guys from the Grease band, who were waiting for Joe Cocker to arrive, when I spotted the unmistakable figure of Janis [Joplin], who was headed in the direction of the catering area. I called out to her and she waved back an acknowledgement, raising the champagne bottle she held in her hand." Lyons hadn't eaten since the night before and was thinking about going over to the catering area when Pete Townshend came striding purposely towards him. "'Leo! Don't eat any of the food, or drink anything that's not from a sealed can. Everything is spiked with acid! I got caught last night.'"

Still photo taken from 8mm film, courtesy Randy Sheets.

"Drug Alley" at Woodstock.

Photo by Barry Melton

Barry Melton of Country Joe and the Fish (right) with Jerry Garcia on stage.

Photo by Jim and Linda Breslin

Exhaustion, acid, or maybe both.

Country Joe's Barry "the Fish" Melton remembers, "I was in the chopper with Joe Cocker, and we were riding low to the trees. It was a heck of a sight. Not only could you see the people in the stage area, you could see that there were another several hundred thousand people in the trees beyond the fringe. That's when I realized how many people were actually there."

Randy Sheets recalls a long lull after Jefferson Airplane. "We walked up the hill and over to a wooded area referred to as Hippie Lane and Drug Alley. There we found folks set up on blankets giving out various drugs from LSD to marijuana. There were also makeshift stands set up where people were selling crafts—beads and scarves, tie-dyed clothing, leather goods, and such. We walked back to the hilltop just as a band started into a soulful version of the Beatles:

What would you think if I sang out of tune,
Would you stand up and walk out on me?
Lend me your ears and I'll sing you a song
And I'll try not to sing out of key.
—Lennon/McCartney

Photo by John De Lorenzo

Forever young at Woodstock.

Photo courtesy Clay Borris/www.johnphillipsphotography.com

Looking for a helping hand.

Photo by Cornelius Alexy

"The singer was clad in a tie-dyed t-shirt and seemed to be spazzing out as he sang. It was Joe Cocker. We never heard of him or his music, but his sound and band were amazing!"

Patrick Howe recalls, "As Joe Cocker's set progressed, the wind began to pick up, and we became aware of the sky quickly changing. It seemed as if he was summoning up the tempest with his wild performance, and just as his set ended, a huge thunderstorm hit. I was struggling to get up the hill when someone stuck a camera in my face and backwards I fell in the mud.

Photo by Cornelius Alexy

Joe Cocker summons a storm.

Photo by Derek Redmond and Paul Campbell

A crowd closely watches Cocker—and the skies.

Photo by Cornelius Alexy

Muddied blankets in the sun after the torrential downpour.

Photo by Cornelius Alexy

Finding a dry patch of ground, dry blanket to sit on, or dry anything was a challenge.

Photo by Cornelius Alexy

The top plateau concession area, littered and muddy.

For Jackie Watkins, the thought of rain was daunting, but her friend, Eric, came prepared with a huge plastic sheet to wrap their stuff in, and sure enough the rains came—torrential rains. "We got soaked to the bone. There was mud everywhere, and it was spraying everywhere. The towers were swaying, and people were screaming, scrambling for cover. The greatest fear was those towers coming down. There were fools climbing up for a better view, and one guy actually fell and had to be air lifted out. The gentlemen who were manning the microphones were very professional but firm. It was much more organized than people think, and not as chaotic as people say."

Photo by John De Lorenzo

A bit of cover during the storm.

Photo by John De Lorenzo

One man's empty truck is another man's shelter.

Backstage, Ten Years After's Leo Lyons remembers, "The roadies and I huddled in the back of the truck as the drizzle turned into yet another hammering downpour, and the stage was shut down. I later learned that the promoters were in a state of panic. The paths created by the crowd, combined with the rainstorm, had exposed the high voltage cables that brought power to the massive amplification system. The bare wires lay exposed dangerously close to the audience."

Photo by Gary Geyer

"Did somebody call my name?"

Photo by Gary Geyer

Photo by Gary Geyer

"Help me up."

"I remember talk that they were going to shut the whole thing down," recalls Jackie Watkins, "but soon the sun broke through and everything came to life again, and they said we're going to finish this out."

"We got caught in a major downpour with thunder and lightning," remembers Randy Sheets. "A couple of us had stayed back to keep our spot, and the rest of us were quickly flooded out of our leaky tent, so we headed to our car for some much needed rest."

It got really muddy, and some people near where Dennis Himes was standing organized human barrel jumping. Himes recalls, "Some people got down on their hands and knees, side by side, and others would run and leap over them, landing in the mud on the other side.

They were dropping flowers. That was a 'spirit of Woodstock' high point. You're worn out after three days of staying on your feet and keeping awake, and you're just spent—when flowers fall from the sky.

Photo by John De Lorenzo

A National Guard helicopter drops oranges, flowers, and dry clothes.

"We noticed that something was being dropped from of a helicopter. The initial rumor was that it was marijuana," Himes remembers.

"They were dropping flowers," says Trudy Morgal. "That was a 'spirit of Woodstock' high point. You're worn out after three days of staying on your feet and keeping awake, and you're just spent—when flowers fall from the sky. We looked at them for a while and stuck them in our hair. It was wonderful just to have a real, living, beautiful piece of nature that someone cared to provide for you at that time."

Photo by Jim and Linda Breslin

There's always a bit of heaven in a disaster area.
—Wavy Gravy

"The weather turned Woodstock into a national disaster area, and we had a chance to show the world how it would be if we ran the show," says Wavy Gravy. "We surrendered ourselves to this interesting energy, which enabled us to work days without sleep and intuitively pull off stuff that we couldn't have thought about in our wildest dreams. The minute we'd think that it was us doing it, we'd fall on our butt in the mud. So I believe that the universe was acting out. There was this amazing energy that you could surrender to, and it would move you."

On Sunday a surprise guest appeared on his own muddy field. Max Yasgur, known for having a good heart but a poor one in health, came to see what had become of his alfalfa field. Fearing that the site of his farm would be too much for the ailing Max, festival organizers asked if he had any words for the kids. Max took the stage and spoke humbly.

"I'm a farmer…I don't know how to speak to 20 people at one time, let alone a crowd like this. But I think you people have proven something to the world—not only to the Town of Bethel, or Sullivan County, or New York State; you've proven something to the world. This is the largest group of people ever assembled in one place. We had no idea that there would be this size group, and because of that you've had quite a few inconveniences as far as water, food, and so forth. Your producers have done a mammoth job to see that you're taken care of…they'd enjoy a vote of thanks. But above that, the important thing that you've proven to the world is that a half a million kids—and I call you kids because I have children that are older than you are—a half-million young people can get together and have three days of fun and music, and have nothing but fun and music, and God bless you for it!" A roar of applause and approval erupted from Max's once pristine hillside that could be heard for miles.

Photo courtesy Peter J. Corrigan, www.vintagerockandrollphotos.com

In the distance, a farmer is welcomed to the stage.

Harriette Schwartz watches Max Yasgur address the crowd.

Photo by Harriette Schwartz

A half-million young people can get together and have three days of fun and music, and have nothing but fun and music, and God bless you for it!

MAX YASGUR FOR PRESIDENT

That's the way it is, baby

By GIL WEISINGER

BETHEL

"If nominated I will not run -- and if elected I will not serve!"

This sentiment, first expressed by Calvin Coolidge to scotch a move to renominate him for the presidency, is similar to that declared Tuesday by Max Yasgur, the Bethel dairy farmer on whose property the controversial Aquarian Exposition was held in mid-August.

Yasgur, who took the brunt of the blame for the three-day rock and folk fest noted with dismay the increasing campaign by hippies to have him publicized as the darling of the hippie world.

At the forefront of the campaign are a flurry of bumper stickers, in psychedelic colors, proclaiming, "Max Yasgur for President." No one knows the actual source of the campaign, including Yasgur himself, but the stickers were advertised in a recent issue of the New York Times and are being mailed out by the Blue Ribbon Manufacturing Company.

The bumper stickers are now starting to appear in the Sullivan County area, with several observed on passing cars driven by the "over 30 generation."

But Max, as he is affectionately known to those who grooved on the grass is not only a reluctant candidate but quietly asserts his privilege to privacy.

Max Yasgur

Considered a usually cooperative man with the news media, Yasgur said Tuesday he recently contacted his attorney Hyman C. Levine of Jeffersonville in an effort to determine what could be done to stop the unauthorized use of his name Levine he said, is currently probing the legal angle

He emphatically contends the use of his name on the stickers was not authorized by him and denounced the presidential drive in no uncertain terms

Yasgur said he first became aware of the campaign when he observed the bumper stickers in New York over the weekend Adding to his political favor, is the wealth of publicity he received in the form of a picture and story in Life Magazine s special edition about the festival and from prominent stories in major newspapers in the nation

In being named for the presidency although claiming his unwillingness Yasgur joins the ranks of others nominated by hippiedom Louis Abolafia a Greenwich Village hippie who specializes in locating runaways for distressed parents, was the candidate in 1964

Abolafia was shown nude on posters with the campaign slogan enscribed I have nothing to hide

Yasgur also has the dubious distinction of sharing the hippie's candidate list with a pig, nominated in 1968 by the Hog Farm, a New Mexico commune

While the actual reason for the campaign to promote Yasgur is not known, among the possibilities is that he incurred the favor of the younger generation in his approach to their sometimes socially-unacceptable antics

Other reasons are that the firms printing the posters and stickers stand to make a considerable amount of money, and that the festival promoters may want to keep the memory of the event alive in order to cash in on future ventures

Among those known locally to have purchased the bumper stickers is Monticello pharmacist Emil C Motl who said he wanted them because he knows Max and Mimi and thought the stickers would make a nice keepsake

In a way, Motl is not unlike the legions of souvenir hunters who raided the Bethel site after the festival seeking artifacts, or the many thousands who bought copies of everything written about the locally-historic event

Photo by Patricia Salamone

Patricia Salamone looks at a muddy crowd from under a makeshift shelter.

"The landscape now resembled a quagmire of sludge," says Stu Fox. He recalls that the once enormous crowds were gone with the wind, driven away by the deluge. "I spent that night on top of a crane alongside the stage. Ten Years After, Johnny Winter, and Crosby, Stills, Nash and Young shined Sunday night, but the Paul Butterfield Blues Band was the highlight of my trip aboard the crane. The 'Love March' was a real surprise, being much more attuned to the Woodstock crowd than their usual blues songs."

For Artie Kornfeld, Sunday was in full swing. He and company had put up the best acts for three solid days. Country Joe and the Fish had just entertained the soggy masses with their blend of politically satirical rock and soul music.

"I asked for something to help keep me awake," Kornfeld remembers. "My wife, Linda, and I were given what we were told were diet pills, but instead were THC and acid mixed together." Kornfeld had never taken hallucinogens and was petrified. "I remember sitting on Robbie Robertson's [The Band] amp, and I started to cry."

The rains had knocked out the turntable on the stage that would have allowed them to set up a new band as one was playing, and he watched as the stage crew lugged amps, trying to really keep the festival moving. "They truly had their hearts into this," he remembers. Though it was a beautiful thing, Artie began to hallucinate, experiencing his first bum trip. "I started thinking about all the bad things that might have happened," Artie remembers. "I was seeing the bridge from the stage over the road to the performers' area on fire. I was thinking that the National Guard was rappeling down ropes from the helicopters into the crowd and attacking everyone. The essence of my experience was caught in the lines of Joni's [Mitchell] 'Woodstock.'"

And I dreamed I saw the bombers
Riding shotgun in the sky
And they were turning into butterflies
Above our nation
—Joni Mitchell

Still photo taken from 8mm film, courtesy Randy Sheets.

Photo by Lynn Spencer

Taking a shortcut from the lake to the campground.

Singer Joe Crocker of England, foreground, stands at the stage before a performance with the masses of fans spread out before him in the Aquarian amphitheater. --TH-Record photo

Rain triggers early exodus, but not for all

(Continued from Page 1)
doctors were flown from New York City and 11 helicopters were hired to ferry in medical supplies and additional food and beverages. Several dozen drug and accident victims were airlifted to area hospitals.

Three mild cases of hepatitis were reported Sunday, raising fears of infectious diseases spawned by the ghetto conditions in this temporary tent city of 450,000.

Between acts of the greatest array of musical stars ever assembled for a rock-folk festival, an announcer Saturday reported 300 cases of "bad acid," meaning LSD and other hallucinogens, and warned the audience to avoid both green and blue pills. Cases continued to roll in to the nine on-site medical stations Sunday.

One youth, who reportedly set himself afire by accident, was airlifted to a local hospital Sunday. At least three births and four miscarriages occurred.

As of early Sunday evening, police had arrested more than 300 on narcotics charges. Festival-based police accounted for 77, most of these nearby, not on premises, and mostly for sale or felonious possession of drugs. Other arrests were of drug-laden festival-goers en route.

State and local police on site evidently had been under orders to arrest only for crimes of violence, ignoring drugs, according to gleanings from lower-echelon law enforcers willing to speak without being named.

The Times Herald-Record staff on site, augmented by estimates from informed medical and other observers, had made its own evaluation of the extent of drug use:

At least 80 per cent -- perhaps 90 -- used marijuana during the festival. At least 50 per cent used hallucinogens like LSD and mescaline or mood-alterers like the amphetamines ("uppers" in the parlance) and tranquilizers ("downs").

The drug traffic problem can be expected to continue in the encampment that remains deep into this week and early next.

Fears of violence, riot, and crowd control problems undoubtedly underlay the unofficial hands-off attitude, judging by comments of lawmen.

And, barring a few incidents, the policy paid off. The crowds remained ruly. Raids on concession tents during "Hungry Saturday" were kept within bounds. A rumored commando raid on the performers' food tent -- where champagne was on the posh menu while other festival-goers scrounged for food and water -- did not materialize Saturday night.

Traffic heavy, moving

MIDDLETOWN

At 9:30 p.m. Sunday, state police said traffic on the Rt. 17 Quickway and the Thruway was heavy but moving freely.

"It's not bumper-to-bumper yet," one trooper said. "It's about the same as most Sunday nights."

Two accidents were reported, including one involving a bus, but no serious injuries resulted, according to police.

Photo courtesy Peter J. Corrigan, www.vintagerockandrollphotos.com

© Elliott Landy/Landyvision.com

Leo Lyons keeps the rhythm during Ten Years After's set.

After a visit to the hospital tent and a dose of Thorazine, Sunday prematurely ended for Artie.

Alvin Lee of Ten Years After was a lean and hungry Brit whose guitar looked like it would tip him over. Leo Lyons remembers, "It was about 8 p.m. when we took to the stage, and the pools of water mirrored the lights; the crowds at the immediate front were glistening from the light being reflected off their wet clothes. Further back up the hill was like looking out on a thrumming mass of black molasses interspersed with the occasional glow from a fire, and in the spotlights I could see a steamy mist rising up in the night air. We could certainly feel the energy and warmth from the people. I knew we had tuning problems due to the humidity but nobody cared." Ten Years After blew everybody away with a rocking set that concluded with their monumental "I'm Goin' Home," and Alvin Lee left the stage with a massive watermelon on his shoulders.

Johnny Winter from Beaumont, Texas, was 25 when asked to play at Woodstock. "We knew it was going to be a big happening and it was something we wanted to be part of," says Winter. "People say that if you can remember Woodstock, you weren't there. Well, I'm here to say the memories are very blurry, but I was there. I do know that we were flown to the site by helicopter, Uncle John Turner (drums), Tommy Shannon (bass) and I, and actually given Jimi's spot at 12:30 a.m. Sunday. I can remember how clear the skies were that night and how enormous the crowd was." Winter tore into his distinctive Texas sound, electrifying the crowd with gems that included "Tobacco Road" and "Mean Town Blues."

Photo by Derek Redmond and Paul Campbell

A hillside of mud.

Photo by David Marks (3rd Ear Music/Hidden Years Music Archives 1969-2009)

The Band.

Jackie Watkins recollects how her friend, Eric, had alluded all weekend that she was in for some kind of surprise, and she remembers being quite anticipatory. "I remember early Sunday morning Eric blindfolded me and sat behind me with his hands on my shoulders. At about 4 a.m., he handed me his powerful binoculars, released the blindfold, and said, 'This is my surprise to you. There's your angel,' and there he was—Stephen Stills—a blonde man wearing a blue and white poncho and a yellow shirt, a big gold watch, and a pair of tight jeans."

Watkins sat there, mesmerized. "He took my breath away. I will never forget the most immortal lines, when Stephen said, 'Thanks, we needed that. This is our second gig, man, and we're scared shitless.'" Crosby, Stills, Nash and later, Young, could have been called a new super group as it was a combination of the best music the late '60s offered: The Hollies, The Byrds, Buffalo Springfield, melding their harmonies together. For most, it was the first time hearing "Suite: Judy Blue Eyes" and "Guinevere."

Photo courtesy Clay Barris/www.johnphillipsphotography.com

Keef Hartley Band takes the stage early in Saturday's lineup.

Photo courtesy Peter J. Corrigan, www.vintagerockandrollphotos.com

Trying to get dry after Sunday's storm.

Photo courtesy Peter J. Corrigan, www.vintagerockandrollphotos.com

Crowds thin following torrential downpours.

Still photo taken from 8mm film, courtesy Randy Sheets.

Attendees volunteered to pick up garbage. The by-product of human inhabitation was too much to keep up with.

"It was misty—rainy, misty, and very cold," recalls Watkins. "I remember David asking if they were going to get electrocuted."

As Sunday melted into Monday, The Paul Butterfield Blues Band rounded out Sunday's stellar lineup and ushered in a new day.

"Dawn revealed the garbage-strewn wasteland below us," remembers Stu Fox. Most of the half-million pilgrims to Yasgur's farm had gone home, exhausted but satisfied by their experience. Those who remained were either fast asleep in the mud or continuing their own personal marathon of endurance.

Fox recalls, "The remnants of a once-great army were awaiting the arrival of the psychedelic conqueror, Jimi Hendrix, when the stage suddenly filled with weird-looking people from Sha Na Na, who began setting up their equipment."

Photo courtesy Donny York

Donny York (left) and Jocko Marcellino of Sha Na Na.

Photo courtesy Donny York

Sha Na Na in the early years.

"We kept getting bumped, and we thought that we'd never get on," remembers Jocko. "We didn't get on stage until Monday morning, and the field looked like a refugee camp. We were about to go on, and Paul Butterfield showed up. That's when we said, 'Oh shit, that's it.' So we were almost bumped out of not only Woodstock, but our destiny because that really broke us."

Tommy Hayes, worn out from three days of mud and music, fell asleep and woke up Monday to the music of Sha Na Na and got himself to the stage area. "I remember them so vividly because I was so close. After trying all weekend, I finally made it to the front of the stage and remember thinking it was weird that a '50s band was at this event," says Hayes. "They all dressed in costume."

Sha Na Na hit the stage with some brief mike-checking, hair-combing, and arm-flexing, quickly followed with the instant impact of a drum roll and cymbal crashes, bringing out three synchronized strutting gold guys. "Turned out to be a heck of a wake-up for maybe 40,000 very sleepy freaks," says Donny York.

"I don't believe anyone expected a '50s band," says Joanne Wilson Kelly. "I don't think they had a fan in the audience, but they got a great reception. Everybody was on their feet, dancing around."

People seemed to tighten themselves closer to the stage and abandoned hope of sleeping any later. A few songs into their set, pockets of bare ground were becoming visible some distance out. "I felt let down and yet amused how this was failing to seem like a rock festival. The atmosphere and mood were now more like a Shriners pancake feed than anything necessarily hip," York recalls.

To Donny York, it seemed like their old-time rock and roll show was the ideal final morning arousal for many in the crowd. "I can tell you it was unlike anything else they'd seen on the stage the preceding three days. People who claim to have been there have told me that not everyone was sure they weren't really just sleep-deprived and hallucinating."

Photo courtesy Donny York

Sha Na Na.

Aquarian news briefs

Hospitals at capacity; area doctors alerted

MONTICELLO

At noon Sunday the county's mutual aid center reported that all hospitals were filled. Dr. Sidney P. Schiff of Liberty, who coordinated the physicians' efforts said that some rooms had been left available for major emergencies.

Dr. Lester Lipson of Monticello discosed that hundreds of cases had been treated at the emergency center in Rutherford School.

The injuries and illnesses ranged from cut toes and fingers to the serious reactions from drugs.

All of the county's more than 50 doctors were alerted and pressed into service in various areas. All were on stand-by for emergency calls.

Gordon Winarick, president of the Sullivan County Community General Hospital, disclosed that the hospital had planned for the emergency.

"It was much greater than we anticipated, but our contacts with the medical association and hospitals in Atlantic City and other festival areas, gave us an indication of what to expect." Winarick said.

Hundreds treated at school

MONTICELLO

At the Rutherford School, Dr. Charles Rudiger, Superintendant of Monticello schools, manned a truck to deliver food supplies. School business manager Rubin Pollack also was on the work detail, as were teachers and faculty members in the area.

Dr. Russell Pantel, Monticello School Board president aided at the emergency center, directing the operations in coordinating the effort to care for the hundreds of persons arriving there.

Fourteen men from Stewart Air Force Base were also pressed into service flying the helicopters. A member of the Air Force medical staff, Dr. G. D. Davis, aided in administering to the sick and injured.

Ambulance attendant collapses

MONTICELLO

Thomas Kracht, an ambulance attendant with the Sullivan County Ambulance Service was prostrated from exhaustion. He had worked for 48 hours without rest. After resting for two hours he was back in active duty.

Husband, wife, baby separated

WHITE LAKE

Among the emergencies reported was the separation of a husband, his wife and their two-week-old baby.

Michael Hamilton, 22, of Albuquerque, N.M. told authorities his wife Joanne, 19, had collapsed when she went for water Saturday. She was taken out of the area by ambulance.

Before she went for water she had left her baby with friends. Hamilton had been unsuccessful in locating either his wife or baby.

He said they had come from New Mexico in a truck, which was still at the festival site. He had last seen his wife Saturday afternoon when she went out in the ambulance.

Girl halts speeding vehicle

WHITE LAKE

A petite girl, with blonde hair flowing down to her waist, ran in the road to halt a car speeding down Hurd Road, which was filled with slow-moving hikers shuttling back and forth to the concert area.

She told the driver in unfeminine language what she thought of speeding on a road overflowing with pedestrians.

Referring to the youth who was killed by a tractor, she finished her lecture with, "We already lost a life to wheels. We don't need any more."

Police, fearing a riot, ignore fest drug traffic

WHITE LAKE

Residents of the Catskill Mountain community of White Lake have smiled understandably at just about everything the 450,000 young people have done this weekend at the Woodstock Music and Arts Festival.

But what most area residents cannot understand is why police have ignored the tremendously widespread use of halucinatory drugs by the young people. What they don't know but suspect is that police have been under instructions to do nothing except let the kids do their own thing.

"They told us not to arrest anybody – for anything," said one Rockland County deputy sheriff who was among law enforcement officers from several nearby counties on the grounds. "They said we weren't to make any arrests except in an emergency, like a robbery or an assault."

Because of the arrest-free atmosphere, young people have been openly smoking marijuana and using other halucinogenic drugs, like LSD, mescaline and THC. Marijuana cigarettes have been smoked in front of state troopers.

The groundwork for the hands-off policy was laid several weeks ago by Woodstock security director Wesley F. Pomeroy, a former California undersheriff and member of several presidential crime commissions.

Pomeroy met quietly with top officials of the Federal Bureau of Narcotics and Dangerous Drugs and the State Police Bureau of Criminal Investigation several weeks ago and persuaded them to make no drug arrests on the festival premises.

"We know, of course," Pomeroy said several weeks before the festival, "that if we make even one drug arrest in there (on the grounds) we'll have a major riot on our hands."

The drug scene, despite the fact that anyone using the halucinogenics has considered himself arrest-proof, has been less than happy, however.

Several varieties of LSD have been widely sold -- at $5 for a one trip tablet, $9 for two trips -- all over the grounds.

But most of them, identified by their appearance – blue, green, or green with dots – have proven impure and the number of bad drug reactions has soared.

One doctor reported treating 200 bad-trip patients personally in 24 hours. One first-aid station reported 25 in one hour.

The situation, however, appeared unlikely to change as police continued to smile benevolently on the young people and the youngsters danced in the streets, literally, flying high and feeling groovy.

The Times Herald RECORD

Vol. 14 No. 16 Monday, August 18, 1969

Published every morning, Monday through Saturday by Orange County Publications Division of Ottaway Newspapers-Radio, Inc. 40 Mulberry St., Middletown, N. Y. 10940

Rates: Single copy 10 cents. By carrier, 60 cents a week. By mail in Orange, Sullivan, Ulster, Sussex and Pike Counties, one year $25.00.

Second class postage paid at Middletown, N. Y.

NET PAID CIRCULATION

July 1969 ---------- 44,048

July 1968 ---------- 41,130

Garbage patrol

Two Aquarian festival-goers gingerly handle a load of garbage as they begin to police up the area. The problem of garbage lying all over the festival grounds was becoming critical Saturday. --TH- Record photo by Mike Lee

Nude togetherness on motorcycle built for 3

This is Gene Castellano at White Lake at 9:30: On a crowded section of Hurd Road at the Aquarian Exposition, walkers moved slowly toward a crowded intersection where two state troopers are stationed.

A motorcycle with three riders drove through the crowd to the intersection, turned around, and vanished down a hill toward a swimming area.

Two of the riders, a girl and a boy, were nude.

That's the way it was at the Aquarian Festival.

Aquarian officials predict festival goers to remain

By ETHEL G. ROMM

WHITE LAKE.

Weary Aquarian Exposition officials are already trying to cope with the unexpected set of problems they foresee when the microphones go off after the last guitar strum.

Said one, good-naturedly, "Many of these kids won't leave tomorrow. They're having too much fun. The mountains are too beautiful. We can expect thousands of them to stay on, maybe for a week or two or more. We'll have to feed them, and take care of all the problems in a city of this size, from police and fire protection to hospital care.

"I think this may be the last music festival of this sort. It's too expensive. Unless the performers are willing to donate their time, and the promoters or the community are willing to donate the construction and maintenance costs of running a major metropolis, I don't see how anyone can afford to do this again."

Said another official "It's too bad. You couldn't ask for a happier, nicer, better well-behaved crowd. Maybe one day our society will feel it can afford to sponsor a Festival of Life as quickly as we spend money for wars.

"Right now, we have to think of putting this farm in shape. Our contract says we have two weeks to tear up all the roads we laid and re-seed them and restore the land to its original condition.

"After that, I guess all these sweet kids will just have to leave."

Where in the area will they go to? Communities in California have been trying to cope with child gypsies for several years. Big Sur, Haight Street, and Monterey have all come into everyday vocabulary because of the handling of the problem, and sometimes mis-handling.

The Catskills are different in one telling way: The winters are too cold. With the first chilly winds, the contemporary Children's Crusade, if they have stayed here that long, will head south to the warm deserts of New Mexico and the hot beaches of the West Coast.

index

Chapter 5

"I SEE WE MEET AGAIN." —JIMI HENDRIX ADDRESSES THE WOODSTOCK CROWD

MONDAY, AUG. 18, 1969

Photo by Jean Nichols

Jean Nichols was on the stage and snapped this photo of Jimi Hendrix.

Looking out over the tents and sleeping campers with the sound of Jimi playing was a perfect ending to a perfect concert.

Photo by Gary Geyer

Innocence amongst the trash.

Photo by Jim and Linda Breslin

The grass had been replaced with mud at Woodstock.

"Dawn revealed the garbage-strewn wasteland below us," remembers Stu Fox.

For Caleb Rossiter, James Marshall Hendrix was the fitting wrap-up for Woodstock and the 1960s. It was Monday morning, and the music had gone on all night. Hendrix and his entourage had been flown in, and he sat backstage until it was his time to perform. By this time, the crowd had dwindled to approximately 30,000, and festival-goers could easily approach the stage.

Tommy Hayes recalls the announcement at approximately 8:30 a.m. "I remember when Jimi walked on stage; I tried to work myself down even closer. Seeing Hendrix was 'it' for me. I was mesmerized. Everyone was singing along with the words, while I was struck with awe. My mouth was opened so wide I think my jaw was on the ground. Seeing this guy play guitar the way he did was amazing. He could do what no one else could, and all the hype was being satisfied. Jimi Hendrix was a showman as well as a great guitarist, and it literally blew your mind—seeing it, hearing it, and feeling it."

Lisa Law stepped outside of her tepee to a misty morning after about two hours of sleep. "Looking out over the tents and sleeping campers with the sound of Jimi playing was a perfect ending to a perfect concert."

"I caught the end of the festival from up on the stage, and Jimi looked like a mystic gypsy sorcerer," recalls Sha Na Na's Marcellino. "His guitar danced over, around, and beyond us as his band struggled to keep up."

Photo by David Marks (3rd Ear Music/Hidden Years Music Archives 1969-2009)

Jimi Hendrix mesmerizes the much smaller crowd.

The jam came to a crescendo, and then Jimi blasted into what became his trademark rendition of "The Star Spangled Banner." The twisting and bending of notes brought the century's most turbulent decade and the decade's most famous gathering to a close. It was 10:30 a.m. when the last of Hendrix's notes reverberated through the Catskills. Woodstock was over.

Purple haze all in my brain
Lately things just don't seem the same
Actin' funny, but I don't know why
'Scuse me while I kiss the sky.
—Jimi Hendrix

The top plateau concession area on Monday morning.

Photo by Cornelius Alexy

The Woodstock Nation ends three days of peace and music.

Photo by Cornelius Alexy

The faithful remaining people watch their hero, Jimi Hendrix.

Photo courtesy Peter J. Corrigan, www.vintagerockandrollphotos.com

Everything was everywhere, and the rains had made things wet and worse. "The grass was nothing but a muddy field," recalls Alan Futrell. "I stayed for a while afterwards and participated in the cleanup. I remember our main job was collecting everything that was scattered over the field and then separating it into piles. We found everything from clothes and shoes to backpacks and sleeping bags. Almost anything you could want—or not want."

Jean Nichols and the Hog Farm were responsible for the cleanup and reseeding of Max Yasgur's alfalfa field. "We'd been the cleanup crew for many festivals, but this was unbelievable," says Nichols. "There were masses upon masses of garbage. They actually had to bring in bulldozers to move it. We went around and collected a whole truck full of sleeping bags and brought them down to New York City. Someone paid to have them cleaned, and we gave them away to those who could use them. But there was no chance that a group of us could actually clean that field. I think they had to come in with backhoes and bury everything before they could reseed it and put it back to its pristine condition."

Photo by Cornelius Alexy

All good things must come to an end.

Photo courtesy Clay Barris/www.johnphillipsphotography.com

Concession stands, mud, and garbage as Woodstock ends.

Photo courtesy Peter J. Corrigan, www.vintagerockandrollphotos.com

An embrace marks the end of three days of peace and music.

Photo courtesy Peter J. Corrigan, www.vintagerockandrollphotos.com

Taking it all in, one last time.

Photo by Cornelius Alexy

Watching the final exodus from Yasgur's farm.

Still photo taken from 8mm film, courtesy Randy Sheets.

A last glimpse of "the garden."

Jackie Watkins and her friends also decided to stick around for a while. "Eric was really civic-minded, plus they said that they would pay us if we helped clean up," remembers Jackie. "We were thanked with a goody bag of souvenirs, and we took home around $500. We still had our tickets, and we made a pact to hold onto them as a remembrance of our time we spent together."

Richard Younger was shepherded to a bus and arrived back at the Manhattan Port Authority bus station a few hours later. "When I got there and saw a newspaper, I realized the magnitude of what I had just been part of," he says.

Photo by Stephen Teso

Exhaustion and serenity following the "Woodstock experience."

Photo by Stephen Teso

Stephen Teso, exhausted, on the way home.

Bulldozers, reseeding and replanting in the aftermath of Woodstock.

Photo by Cornelius Alexy

One week after Woodstock.

Photo by Cornelius Alexy

Returning Max's field to its original splendor proved a greater task than originally planned.

Photo by David Marks. (3rd Ear Music/Hidden Years Music Archives 1969-2009)

Final remnants of the Woodstock Nation leave the farm.

Photo by Don Ayers

Barry "the Fish" Melton, Summer of Love Festival, Golden Gate Park, San Francisco, 2007.

Trudy Morgal today admires the current work of Light's designer, Dr. Bob Hieronimus.

"It was more than a musical event," says Fish guitarist Barry Melton. "What you experienced was the ambiance of being there—certainly every bit as much as somebody who was 50 feet from the stage. The point of Woodstock was not what was happening on the stage; the point of Woodstock was that it was a large, spontaneous gathering of young people such as the world had never seen."

Babette Brackett recalls that "whenever we pulled into a rest stop on the Massachusetts Turnpike, we'd see other people wearing six to eight inches of mud on their jeans and have this immediate connection. We would share stories and then continue on our way. It wasn't until we got to Rockport and started talking to our friends and family that we began to realize the enormity of it all."

Tommy Hayes found his ride and headed home. He remembers, "My mother just shook her head when she first saw me. I was a muddy mess and looked exhausted."

"Bob, our driver, took us to his grandmother's house on the way home," remembers Trudy Morgal. "She lived on a lake, and as soon as we got there, we jumped right in. We were so dirty that I expected to see fish popping up dead. We were like the funkiest crew but still having so much fun." Trudy recalls that the newspapers were reporting that the "Woodstock crowd was part of some 'Nightmare in the Catskills.' They insinuated that we caused this big disturbance; that we piled in there and just inundated this little town. Reports made us feel that it was our fault that we caused a spectacle. We felt blame instead of pride in what we just accomplished. At the time, the perception was that we just took over. Took over what?"

Patrick Howe left Woodstock very much altered. He put himself through college and became a punk rock musician and artist in New York.

"Through my years of living in the East Village, I really never mentioned my Woodstock experience until 25 years later,"

Photo by Patrick Howe

Patrick Howe today.

Howe says. *"The New York Times* ran an editorial about the celebration of Woodstock's 25th anniversary, accompanied by a large random shot of the crowd. There, smack dab in the middle of this picture, was me and my friends, Gary Rennie, Dave Babiuk, and Michael Solt."

Greg Henry recalls, "Bob and I went to Woodstock with $20, found a dollar on the ground, and when I got home I had $21 in my pocket. Me and Bob—well, we stayed friends forever, and I wish he was still on this earth. He passed away a few years back, and I miss him very much."

Michael Launder was drafted in July 1972 and conscription ended in December of that year. He remembers that his drill sergeant said to him, "You'll probably be one of the last people to ever be drafted in this country. What's the matter, weren't you smart enough to run off to Canada? Get down and give me 50 just for being stupid."

As Mountain's Felix Pappalardi sang in "Theme For an Imaginary Western," *"Sometimes they found it; sometimes they left it; often lost it along the way."* Landauer says, "At Woodstock, I did all three. Woodstock is where my youth memory resides."

Paul Lehrman, having left after the first day, watched the news reports about the festival and was relieved he didn't stay. In the weeks that followed, he didn't tell too many friends, being a bit embarrassed that he split from what was to be the defining event of his generation. "I've driven up Route 17 many times since August 1969 and passed the exits for White Lake," he says. "Though I don't regret my decision to leave, I can't help but wonder *what if?*"

For Rosemary Forrest, 18, of Jersey City, New Jersey, it was hot. It was humid. It rained. There was limited food, shelter, and creature comforts. There were mosquitoes. And then there was the mud. "It was one of the best times I've ever had," she relates. "We never made it into the concert itself. The crush of people was just too daunting. For this reason people I tell about being at Woodstock often say, 'Oh, but then you weren't actually *there.*' I always correct them. For Woodstock was so much more than just a concert. Most of those who were there didn't attend the concert. The concert wasn't the event—*we* were!"

Less than half of the people trying to get to Woodstock reached their destination. "The police estimated about a million and a half people on the roads who never made it," says Michael Lang. "We had no idea how big the actual community was."

The existing facilities were overwhelmed by those who did make it, and the festival teetered on the edge of disaster all weekend. Torrential rains worsened conditions, but Woodstock survived and managed to flourish during its three-day run. Woodstock thrived in adverse circumstances because people came with strong beliefs. A sense of community made them willing to endure the hardships as many found Woodstock to be a utopian epitome, and many were determined to stay as long as possible. Those days in Bethel left lifelong impressions on those who were there.

"Everything in the universe must have been right where it was supposed to be," says Harriette Schwartz. "Now that I'm older, I realize the horrors that could have transpired, and I have to give everyone there a pat on the back for being so good to each other. The newspapers said otherwise, but we *rocked!*"

Photo by Harriette Schwartz

Harriette Schwartz today.

Photo courtesy Donny York

Donny York (of Sha Na Na) today.

"The myth was that we 'freaks' had demonstrated that we could peaceably share and take care of each other in some sort of socialist utopia model. The fact was," says a now older, realistic Donny York, "we were quite dependent on the life support systems offered by the 'straight' capitalist world outside the festival. They literally rescued us and provided for us to the degree necessary."

York observed that in terms of life support, there was an obvious disaster underway. "Walking around, I encountered nothing but cheerful human warmth, and individuals taking good care of each other. It seemed a time of no competitiveness, only volunteerism and sharing resources. It wasn't socialism at all; there wasn't any people's committee directing anything in top-down fashion; there was just one-on-one caring and patience while we waited for the music despite the delays. It amounted to a *love-in* indeed—not sexualized, just very brotherly, and it felt like heaven. The lesson for the ages wasn't that 'socialism works' [as stated in those urban leftie rags prevalent at the time]; it was that brotherly love really does have a magic power."

Photo courtesy Donny York

Sha Na Na today.

Photo courtesy Walter Parks

Richie Havens remains a vibrant songwriter and performer today.

"I'm glad that I lived through those times. It was a wonderful time for music, for togetherness among people, and for liberation," says Fito de la Parra. "I think it's an era that we should consider as sort of a renaissance period for music, and I don't know if it'll ever be repeated."

"It was like having the windows open, and not knowing what might fly in," recalls Tom Constanten of the Grateful Dead. "It was pretty wild and crazy. You sensed that your perception of time was going rather different; a lot of things were going rather different."

Richie Havens believes that those "who portray the festival in a negative light just don't get it. A lot of what came out of Woodstock was the knack of the press to downgrade the historical factor that it was, and turn it into a sex, drugs, and rock and roll crazy kids scene—which it was not. There were lots of issues flying around."

Havens adds, "There was Vietnam and there were civil rights issues that people felt strongly about, and the coming together was also an expression of those things. It said that people can and do have the right to get together to express themselves peacefully.

"The music was secondary to a large degree," he says. "It was a celebration of people who had believed in something, having a chance to come together and show it as a group. It turned out to be what I call the first American people's festival, meaning that people came out to be with people. It was pretty much a discovery time as well; we all discovered something together.

"There was a vibe, a condition, a sense that Woodstock became," he explains. "I think it was a cosmic accident—the fact that it was a free concert, and that people were free to be themselves. That was the vibe of the day, so we weren't stretching anything at that point."

Photo by Fito de la Parra

Canned Heat's Fito de la Parra with his Woodstock Gold Records.

Photo by Fito de la Parra

Canned Heat's Fito de la Parra's Woodstock Gold Records.

I encountered nothing but cheerful human warmth, and individuals taking good care of each other.

Photo by Nancy Nevins

Nancy Nevins.

Photo by Nancy Nevins

Nancy Nevins performs at the 40th anniversary celebration of the Monterey Pop Festival.

Nancy Nevins was the first woman to sing in a rock band (musicians at that time said women couldn't sing rock). The others were Grace Slick, Janis Joplin, Linda Rondstadt, and Lydia Pence. "We are the vanguard—great- grandmamas of rock, and three of us made it 'Woodstock'," says Nevins. Four months after Woodstock, her career with Sweetwater came to an abrupt end following a head-on collision with a drunk driver. Nevins suffered brain damage and lost the use of a vocal cord. Following years of rehabilitation, she learned to sing again, and she and Sweetwater became the subject of a 1999 VH1 biopic. She is an assistant professor of English at Glendale Community College and Pierce College in Woodland Hills, California, and has continued performing in her own one-woman show and graced the stage at the 40th anniversary celebration of the Monterey Pop Festival.

Photo by Leo Lyons

Leo Lyons of Ten Years After in 2008.

Forty years later, Ten Years After's Leo Lyons is still a working musician who loves what he does. "I feel lucky to have played Woodstock and, although I live in the now, the movie has undoubtedly helped sustain my career," he says. "Many people remember me from those few minutes in the movie and ask what Woodstock was like. I tell them that Woodstock was a good example of something positive that was happening during those times. We wanted to change the world. We had our own ideals, music, and fashions. We imagined a world of love and peace where everyone got along."

Nick Ercoline and Bobbi Kelly were captured on film embraced in a blanket, and that picture has been immortalized as the couple on the front cover of the Woodstock album—with Herbie's butterfly staff seen stuck in the mud. Bobbi points out that the actual picture is somewhat larger, and to her, the better picture can be seen as an oxymoron. To the right of them, lying on the ground, is their friend, Jim Corocran, a Marine who just returned from Vietnam resting peacefully in the field.

Ercoline and Kelly were married in 1971 and returned to Bethel years later on the anniversary of that weekend. "There were people out in the field, camping and celebrating, when we noticed a minivan that had a little fenced area holding two ducks," remembers Kelly. "As we walked by, I said to Nick to go ask what the ducks' names were, and they answered, 'Bobbi and Nick.' We were flabbergasted and, of course, the cuter, smaller duck was Bobbi."

Photo courtesy Joanne Hague

Nick and Bobbi Ercoline today.

Warner Brothers: Woodstock:3 Days of Peace and Music

Nick and Bobbi Ercoline in the famous embrace on the Woodstock LP.

Photo courtesy Chipmonck Archives

Chip Monck today, Victoria, Australia.

E.H.B. (Chip) Monck has been behind the scenes of every major pop-culture event of the last 50 years, from The Village Gate in the early 1960s, the Apollo in Harlem, Newport with Bob Dylan, lighting designer and emcee at Woodstock, losing teeth at Altamont at the hand of a Hells Angel's pool cue, the Rolling Stones' early tours, George Harrison's Concert for Bangladesh, Ali-Foreman's Rumble in the Jungle, The Rocky Horror Show on Broadway, the Los Angeles Olympics, to Pope John Paul at Dodger Stadium. Today, Chip Monck is as busy as ever, providing lighting design for major corporate clients from his home in Australia.

Photo by Lee Levin-Friend

Lee Levin-Friend and her daughters, Kim and Dana (with whom Lee was pregnant while at Woodstock).

Photo by Richard Younger

Richard Younger today.

Photo by Robin Chanin

The Chanins, 2008.

Jackie Watkins and Stephen Stills, 2008.

Photo by Jackie Watkins

Chuck Early today.

Tom Sperry today.

In 1993, Tom Sperry was living in Los Angeles. He had an old Fender amp that he didn't have much use for, so he decided to sell it. He put an ad in the paper, and he received a response from John Fogerty's manager. This fellow said Fogerty was recording in a studio nearby and asked if he could bring it over for John to try. Of course Sperry said he would. They sat through a private concert as John checked out the amp. Sperry told Fogerty that CCR was the reason they went to Woodstock, and he proceeded to tell him his tale.

[Fogerty] said that when CCR finally got on stage, all he could see were bodies scattered everywhere. He said he never forgot when some guy about a hundred yards away, holding a lit lighter over his head, yelled out something like, "Far out, John!" He said the weirdest thing was that he heard the guy perfectly from that distance. Sperry happened to have his Woodstock poster in the car, and he asked if Fogerty would mind signing it. Fogerty said it would be an honor and included Sperry's wife's name even though she didn't attend the event. It [the poster] reads, "Cathy and Tom, nice seeing you again. J C Fogerty."

In 1994, Trudy Morgal remembers that the papers were running stories and pictures for the 25th anniversary. "I always look at pictures from Woodstock, trying to find somebody I recognize. This day, I opened the center section of a Maryland newspaper, and there was a full-page picture of me and Rick! I never dreamt I would actually see *me* in a picture."

Could Woodstock ever happen again? Morgal doesn't think so.

"How can you do twice what nobody planned to do once, or make something happen when it didn't happen on purpose? I don't believe you can do it now. The general mindset is too paranoid, there are too many rules, too many 'what ifs,' and it goes right back to the people. The people who put on the show had a great vision and they handled it well, but then…they had a great group of people—everybody's heart was in the right place. In retrospect, I wish it were like that again. What we had was great but it wasn't appreciated. We just thought it would always be that way."

In the years to follow, Tommy "Purple" Hayes returned to Bethel for the 5th, 10th, 15th, and 20th anniversaries and every year since. Hayes discovered his love for drumming at Woodstock. He was inspired by Santana and his percussionists, and has carried that passion with him ever since.

Donald Murphy, 27, from Cincinnati, remembers volunteering at the "Bad Trip Tent." Sometime in the late 1990s, he was visiting a stone carver's studio in Llano, New Mexico. The artist's wife was serving tea, and there was a picture of a girl on a Woodstock poster. Murphy asked if it was her, and she said yes, that she and her partner were there. He was a member of the New York Fire Department at the time. They went to enjoy the concert, but also to do what they could to help out. Murphy told her about his experience.

"Soon after her partner came in, and I described the tent area as best I could, and he says, 'Damn, it's a small world!' George Carlin said [in part], 'We can send a man to the moon, but we can't cross the street to shake a new neighbor's hand.' There were a lot of new neighbors to shake hands with in those days at Woodstock. So many beautiful people."

Photo by Tommy Hayes

Tommy Hayes today.

Upon returning to work at Warner Bros., a couple of head honchos always took the opportunity to tease Harriette Schwartz during screenings of the Woodstock movie. They'd say, "Isn't that you shaving your armpits in the lake??" As for Alan from the mailroom, he and Harriette strung some beads and had a few more dates, but eventually went their separate ways.

Christopher Cole made the decision to return home on Sunday. He and his new friend, Maria, arrived the next morning in Tarrytown. It was a beautiful warm summer day.

"As I left Maria on the corner, I thanked her for the weekend and for what we shared. A week later I received a gift. She sent me a beautiful gold St. Christopher's medal inscribed, 'Love Always, Maria 8-28-69.' It hangs from my neck to this day."

Months passed, but Cole's memory of that woman did not. "I couldn't get her out of my mind. One day I cranked up the bike, rode into Tarrytown, and looked her up," he says. "This June 28 (2009) will be our 39th wedding anniversary."

Christopher Cole, his wife Maria, and Duke Devlin (seated) are all Woodstock alumni.

Photo by John De Lorenzo

John De Lorenzo today.

Photo by Don Aters

Tom Constanten (Grateful Dead), Don Aters, and Paul Kantner (Jefferson Airplane), 2007.

Jahanara Romney and Wavy Gravy today at their Camp Winnarainbow.

Jean Nichols today.

Photo by Jean Nichols

John Rossi sums it up by saying, "Woodstock left me never to be the same again. It's a place I carry with me wherever I go. I guess in some ways, you can take me out of Woodstock, but you can't take Woodstock out of me."

Woodstock was also a life-changing event for Jahanara Romney. "I was working very hard, but I didn't have credentials to be working in the medical tents and feeding thousands of people. I wouldn't have been allowed to do anything like that in my outer life, but I did it very well. I saw all of us hippies from the Hog Farm working our butts off, and we were magnificent. I realized that if we were in charge of the world, we'd do a mighty fine job!"

It changed her views of how she saw herself, and what she perceived the Hog Farm to be. "I knew we were pretty competent, but up until then, I wasn't feeling important or contributing," she says. "After Woodstock I realized I was good at what I was doing, and so was Wavy, and everyone else from the Hog Farm."

Romney and Wavy Gravy went on to support many social causes, including the SEVA Foundation, which supports projects in the areas of health and wellness, community development, environmental protection, and cultural preservation. They also founded Camp Winnarainbow, a circus and performing arts camp for children and adults in California.

Photo by Jean Nichols

One of the Hog Farm's painted buses 40 years after Woodstock.

Photo by Jean Nichols

The Hog Farm's "Road Hog" 40 years after the pilgrimage to Woodstock.

Photo by Patricia Salamone

Patricia Salamone today.

Patricia Salamone left Woodstock that Sunday and never went back to church. "After Woodstock, I discovered that *church* was everywhere to me. Also, at Woodstock I learned that having the right clothes and makeup didn't mean that much anymore. That was the 'outside' and it's what's 'inside' that counts."

Photo by Don Aters

(Jefferson Airplane) Marty Balin, Summer of Love Festival, Golden Gate Park, San Francisco, 2007.

Photo by Don Aters

Country Joe, Summer of Love Festival, Golden Gate Park, San Francisco, 2007.

"As I drove away from the meeting of the counterculture, I had seen the best that it had to offer, and the many ways one could choose to respond to the challenges of the time," Caleb Rossiter reflects on his experience. "After Woodstock I chose to not 'drop out' with Timothy Leary, not go up to the country with Canned Heat, not sit back and groove on a rainy day or live in Electric Ladyland with Jimi Hendrix. I left Woodstock energized, still believing that we could help in the real world—help end war and injustice. I learned at Woodstock, and as Joe Cocker declared on stage amidst the growing tempest around him, '[We could all] get by with a little help from our friends.'"

Photo by Don Aters

(Jefferson Airplane) Paul Kantner, Summer of Love Festival, Golden Gate Park, San Francisco, 2007.

Chapter 6

THE LEGACY OF WOODSTOCK

Following Woodstock, Max Yasgur continued to support the generation he hosted, listening to their issues and providing his fatherly guidance. He was even touted as the generation's presidential nominee, though he graciously declined the accolade.

Two years after the concert, he toured Israel and had the opportunity to meet Israel's first prime minister, David Ben-Gurion. As Ben-Gurion went down the receiving line, "Max said, 'I'm Max Yasgur of Bethel,' and Ben-Gurion shakes his hand and says, 'Oh yeah, that's where Woodstock was, wasn't it?'" says Liberty's Lou Newman, a friend of Yasgur. In February 1973, the world lost a good man when Max Yasgur succumbed to a heart attack at the early age of 53.

In a deal brokered by Artie Kornfeld three days before the festival, Woodstock was guaranteed immortality through the 1970 release of a Warner Bros. documentary on the three-day festival. It also received the 1970 Academy Award for "Best Documentary." Woodstock would become forever revered as both the yin and yang of what the '60s youth represented.

Following Max Yasgur's death in '73, Louis Nicky from Brooklyn bought the 40-acre Woodstock concert bowl from Mariam Yasgur, Max's wife. Twice, the town put up a sign identifying Nicky's land as the site of the event. Twice, the sign was stolen.

Photo by Barry Smith

Hurd and West Shore Road.

Photo by Barry Smith

The field and monument to Woodstock.

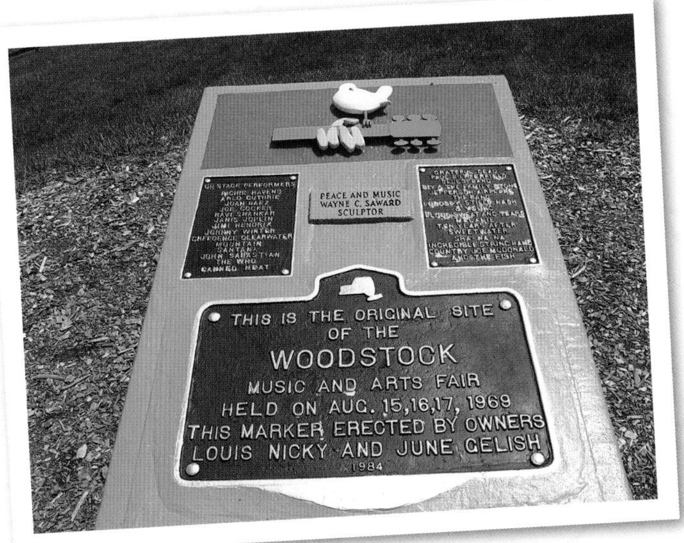

Photo by Barry Smith

Woodstock monument.

For years, no one celebrated Woodstock's anniversary, and August came and went without notice. With the lack of any identifiable markers, people who did travel to reminisce at Yasgur's farm weren't always sure of being at the right place.

In the late 1970s, a ragtag bunch started celebrating every August with a three-day reunion at the original site. In 1978, a welder named Wayne Saward came out for the party. "It was like super-quiet," he recalls. "There'd be 30 people there, at most. And that was in the middle of the night." Then in 1984, Saward built the world's only monument to the event. It's a 5-1/2-ton marker made of cast iron and concrete, subsidized by landowner Louis Nicky. The marker was put in place for the 15th anniversary, and the site became a counterculture shrine. Visitors from around the globe started showing up randomly, staying for a few minutes, then leaving, and that pilgrimage continues today.

Woodstock's 10th Anniversary Festival

Ball State University's Michael Wm. Doyle, Ph.D., a counterculture historian, describes how over the past three decades various parties have staged, or attempted to stage, successors to Woodstock. They have taken place either by that name at different sites or else on or near the original site under a different name—some more commercial than others. The first festival held in homage to Woodstock occurred around the 10th anniversary date in 1979 at Parr Meadows in Long Island. This concert included veterans Canned Heat, John Sebastian, Country Joe, Johnny Winter, Stephen Stills, and others. It was reportedly a flop.

Canned Heat.

Country Joe McDonald.

Stephen Stills.

Photos by Bob Sanderson

John Sebastian.

Johnny Winter.

Paul Butterfield.

Photos by Bob Sanderson

A House on Yasgur Road

Max Yasgur's home.

The last piece of Max Yasgur's farm.

Photo by Joanne Hague

In 1985, Miriam Yasgur decided to sell their homestead. It was purchased by Roy Howard, a Monticello, New York resident and Woodstock alumnus. A stipulation in the deed stated that one square foot of land would remain Yasgur property, ensuring that a piece of Max's farm would forever remain.

Max's house and calving barn can still be seen from Highway 17B heading toward Bethel, New York.

For the 25th anniversary, two competing commercial concerts were planned. One was billed as Woodstock '94 (or "Woodstock II"). It was held in Saugerties, New York, a Hudson River town just east of Woodstock, coincidentally one of the locations where Woodstock Ventures first considered holding the 1969 event. It was promoted as the Woodstock that would make money, in part through corporate sponsorship, better security, and the advance sale of audio, film, and broadcast rights. Despite these preparations, a crowd numbering at least 200,000 overwhelmed the gates on the first day and managed once again to turn Woodstock into a free festival by default.

A different festival was also planned at the original Yasgur farm site. "Bethel '94"—a festival produced by Shea Entertainment/Sid Bernstein Ltd., the man who brought the Beatles to the United States. Despite the fact that the concert was cancelled in early August due to poor ticket sales, more than 25,000 fans showed up anyway. They were freely entertained by musicians who had played at the first festival, including Richie Havens, Country Joe McDonald, Arlo Guthrie, Canned Heat, Sha Na Na, and Melanie. Following this gathering, a resurgence of interest in Woodstock and celebrating its anniversary in Bethel spread, much to the chagrin of local authorities.

25,000 show up on the original Woodstock site in 1994 for the 25th anniversary.

Photo by John Straub

The little drummer boy.

Photo by John Straub

Everyone just came again. Aug. 13, 1994.

Photo by John Straub

This troupe of folks had the kids in a state of awe. A real gas.

Photo by John Straub

Accommodations in all shapes and sizes at the 25th anniversary in Bethel, New York.

Photo by John Straub

Woodstock alumni Melanie takes the makeshift stage for the first of two performances.

Photo by John Straub

Melanie performs for a second time.

"Well, I missed it," says Doug Mowrey of Pittsburgh. "I was as close as the NYC Port Authority Terminal where all these strange-looking people were getting on buses headed for 'some sort of music festival'. I had just received my discharge from the Army in June and at the time, I had no idea what was unfolding and neither did the world. It wasn't until three days later when I realized what I had missed. Woodstock… and to think that I could have jumped on one of those buses."

Fast-forward 25 years; the plans for Woodstock II in Saugerties, New York, were in full swing. "Reading about that event did nothing to excite me," Mowrey tells. "I was 52 then and not about to travel from Pittsburgh to mingle with the Pepsi generation. I was more interested about the reunion concert on the original site of Yasgur's farm, but I read that those plans fell through, and unfortunately, was cancelled.

"But here's where the spirit of Woodstock transcends human understanding," says Mowrey. "I told my wife that I was going to drive to Bethel for the anniversary anyway, just to see if anybody shows up at the original site to commemorate the event. I set out on my adventure, not knowing exactly where I was heading, or having any idea where the site was located. I remember that, as I drove, I wondered that if I find the original site, was I going to feel like a damn fool if I'm the only soul in that natural amphitheatre. But onward I went. As fate would have it, I stopped for gas at a country store that was selling a local paper running a commemorative edition about Woodstock. The paper included a map of the festival site, and now I knew where I was going.

Photo by John Straub

Pass the boy! People were really gentle. It's Woodstock, after all.

Photo by John Straub

"Mountain" Noel Redding, Corky Laing and Leslie West play Woodstock 25 years later on an impromptu-built stage.

Photo by John Straub

Arlo Guthrie makes his return to Woodstock.

"When I reached Hurd Road, a state police car was parked and I thought, 'This is a good sign,' turned left and continued up a hill. At the top looking down, I couldn't believe my eyes. There were tepees, tents, and people. Hundreds of people, and this was only Friday afternoon. I drove down to the intersection and passed a small stage made from two-by-fours and plastic tarp. I pitched my tent while I could still find space and settled in for three days of a most wonderful experience. I wasn't the only soul in that amphitheater and by that night, there were endless lines of headlights backed up all over the hills.

"Saturday, three of four flatbed trailers were brought in and parked side by side to make a larger stage, and the sound system followed with speaker banks on both sides of the flatbeds. This was one of those 'if we build it, they will come' spiritual journeys...and come they did. For a non-event, there had to be 100,000 people that came to remember, celebrate, and listen to the music. There were several of the original Woodstock acts that showed up and played for free.... Arlo Guthrie, Melanie, Richie Havens, Country Joe McDonald, Mountain, and oh yeah, we had our rain and mud too–like the heavens 'knew' what to do and when to do it.

"That trip will be a lasting memory for me. I was moved beyond words. Now I know the spirit of Woodstock, and it does live on!"

For over 10 years Roy and Jeryl welcomed pilgrims back to Max's farm for three-day celebrations that often included stages with music performances, mini-stages for jam sessions, drum circles, free kitchens, and camping. "Woodstockers," as we were called, were always "Welcomed Home."

Photo by John Straub

Everything is possible at Woodstock.

Gerry Bernicky, Toronto, Canada

Everywhere was a song and a celebration.

Gerry Bernicky, Toronto, Canada

Toronto's Gerry Bernicky getting an early start at the Woodstock 33rd anniversary reunion hosted by Roy Howard and Jeryl Abramson.

Woodstock anniversary "reunions" find a new home at Max's homestead four miles up the road.

Gerry Bernicky, Toronto, Canada

One of many drum circles over the reunion weekend.

In 1996, Liberty, New York, cable billionaire Alan Gerry (of the Gerry Foundation Inc.) purchased the Woodstock property along with more than 1,400 surrounding acres. Gerry's vision was to create a performing arts center on 650 acres of that property, which would include several music performance pavilions, theaters, a performing arts school, and music museum. After the Woodstock site was sold, the annual reunions were halted by Gerry, with the help of the town board. People were no longer allowed to celebrate on that land.

Roy Howard and his wife, Jeryl Abramson, who now own the Yasgur homestead, stepped in to help. They welcomed the celebrants to their farm—Max's farm. Thousands of pilgrims from all over the world would make the trek to Roy and Jeryl's to celebrate Woodstock's anniversary. The reunions continued every August for the next 10 years, until the town permanently enjoined the couple from welcoming people. In 2006, after years of controversy and legal battles, the annual gatherings were banned by the Town of Bethel through the use of excessive police force, but the people still come.

Photo courtesy Joanne Hague

Petition document submitted to the Joint Lead Agency for the Performing Arts Center, Bethel, New York, Sept. 12, 2002. The request for nomination to the 11 Most Endangered Historic Places in the U.S. for 2003 (three parts), submitted to the National Trust for Historic Preservation, Jan. 20, 2003. A Cause for Preservation submitted to the Town of Bethel Planning Board, April 6, 2004.

In mid-August 1999, the Gerry Foundation held a commercial concert, the first at the site since 1969. Known as "A Day in the Garden," it headlined Don Henley, Lou Reed, Joni Mitchell, and Stevie Nicks, and featured Ten Years After, Pete Townsend, Richie Havens, Melanie, and John Sebastian. Alternative groups such as the Goo Goo Dolls and Third Eye Blind also played to the audience that cumulatively numbered 79,000 over the three days. The Gerry Foundation followed up this concert the following summer, with a one-day show featuring nine performers, five of whom had played the 1969 festival.

The previous month, Woodstock '99, organized by Michael Lang and John Scher, was held at the former Griffiss Air Force Base in Rome, New York. Despite high ticket prices and a setting that was the antithesis of Yasgur's farm, the festival managed to attract more than 220,000 young people. Attendees were treated to a stellar lineup of primarily alternative, rock, and pop groups on three stages, programmed simultaneously. A summer heat wave coupled with what many festival-goers considered gouging prices ($4 for bottled water), the festival ended with rioting and arson. Nearly all of the sensationalized news coverage contrasted this debacle with the more specific, although equally stressed, crowd at the original festival.

Along with the ambitious plans for Bethel Woods came those who questioned and challenged them. The once-known freedom of the open field was now compromised by fencing, concrete barriers, visiting hours, and security patrols. By 1998, an assembly of people known as The Friends of Yasgur's Farm had grown out of concern and opposition to what was taking place in Bethel. From that group, the grassroots Woodstock Preservation Alliance was born. The group's mission was to preserve the Woodstock site as an open field, where all would be welcome for generations to come, and it paved the way for the efforts that followed.

Though concerns were valid, the Alliance's efforts to thwart development were more local in nature, which reduced their effectiveness. The spring of 2002 brought with it plans for the construction of Bethel Woods—Center for the Performing Arts, and with it an evolution in the preservation efforts. Through the leadership of the authors of this book, Brad Littleproud and Joanne Hague, with support from Woodstock alumni such as festival co-creator Artie Kornfeld, an advanced historic preservation campaign emerged. Efforts included attempts to have the original Woodstock site listed on the National Trust for Historic Preservation—11 Most Endangered Places in America [USA]; formal requests to the owners for the submission of an application for the site to be placed on the National Register of Historic Places; and formally submitted arguments challenging the Woodstock site's development plans with respects to New York state and federal preservation laws. With a steady, unabashed dose of pressure, changes to the plans for Bethel Woods included a much smaller footprint of buildings on the upper plateau. The bowl itself was left untouched. Though considered an unwelcome watchdog, the Alliance demonstrated that, with perseverance and using the very systems that threatened the Woodstock site, the voice of the people could be heard.

Photo courtesy Sullivan County Democrat, Ted Waddell, photographer

Challenging the plans for the development of the Woodstock site, Joanne Hague of the Woodstock Preservation Alliance issues a statement to the Bethel town planning board.

Photo © Marvin S. Baum, Baum Image Group, Inc., www.BaumImageGroup.com

Display with newspaper headlines, photographs, the Woodstock record album, and Yasgur Farms milk bottle.

Photo © Marvin S. Baum, Baum Image Group, Inc., www.BaumImageGroup.com

A new generation checks out Woodstock producer Michael Lang's BSA motorcycle seen in the Woodstock documentary (Warner).

On June 19, 2004, the exhibit "Spirit of the Woodstock Generation: The Photographs of Elliott Landy" opened at the New York State Museum in Albany, commemorating the 35th anniversary of the 1969 Woodstock Festival. This exhibition featured more than 50 original photographs by Elliott Landy, official photographer of the Woodstock Festival, in addition to Woodstock memorabilia contributed by Woodstock personalities and attendees.

About one year earlier, Elliott had met Marvin Baum and mentioned to him that there were no major events planned to commemorate the 35th anniversary, which gave Baum the idea to spearhead this project himself.

Working from his kitchen table in Rockland County, New York, with just a telephone and laptop computer, Baum set out to create and organize a major celebration centered around an exhibition of Landy's iconic images. Initially, he attempted to contact the Brooklyn Museum as a possible venue, but his calls were never returned. After that, Baum contacted the New York State Museum, which greeted his ideas enthusiastically.

Photo courtesy Brad Littleproud

Original Woodstock artist Melanie following her performance at the opening night of the exhibit.

Photo © Marvin S. Baum, Baum Image Group, Inc., www.BaumImageGroup.com

Woodstock promoter Artie Kornfeld (left), Woodstock performer John Sebastian (center), and Marvin Baum (right), Woodstock 35th Anniversary creator/organizer.

The opening reception, which was held on June 22, officially kicked off the summer-long celebration at the museum. This event was attended by Woodstock organizers Michael Lang and Artie Kornfeld as well as Woodstock performers John Sebastian and Melanie.

Afterward, New York Governor George Pataki hosted a special Woodstock anniversary dinner at the executive mansion, where both Sebastian and Melanie performed for the governor and his guests, who sat casually on the floor of the mansion's living room.

On Aug. 12, the museum held a panel discussion, "Woodstock: The Music, the People and the Times," with Woodstock organizers Michael Lang and Joel Rosenman among the panelists. There was also a concert series featuring musicians who performed on the 1969 Woodstock stage, including John Sebastian, Melanie, Arlo Guthrie, Jefferson Airplane, and others, evoking the music that made Woodstock famous.

Photo © Marvin S. Baum, Baum Image Group, Inc., www.BaumImageGroup.com

Display with an original festival site map drawing (top), clothes worn by attendees and crew shirts and jackets (below).

Photo © Marvin S. Baum, Baum Image Group, Inc., www.BaumImageGroup.com

Display with Woodstock program, Life magazine, ticket, photograph, and hat worn at Woodstock.

Photo © Marvin S. Baum, Baum Image Group, Inc., www.BaumImageGroup.com

Joel Rosenman (left) and Michael Lang, Woodstock producers, at a panel discussion.

Photo © Marvin S. Baum, Baum Image Group, Inc., www.BaumImageGroup.com

Woodstock performer Arlo Guthrie (center) and Elliott Landy (right), Woodstock photographer.

"I wore my 'maverick' jacket to Woodstock, and I wish I had a photo of me in it," says Scott A. Munroe. "You don't know how many times I almost trashed this thing over the years, but I never could. It's my Woodstock relic."

Photo courtesy James Riley

Concrete stage blocks and footings, unearthed while constructing the stage for the "Day in the Garden" festival in 1998, are a few of the remaining artifacts of the festival.

Photo courtesy Scott A. Munroe

Denim "maverick" jacket worn at the Woodstock festival.

Banner left hanging at the site of Woodstock.

Photo by Francis Cardamone

Banner found on Monday.

Photo by Francis Cardamone

"Who made them?" wonders Francis Cardamone. These flags, hung two on a cross-pole, were "saved" by Cardamone as he departed from the Woodstock concert site on Monday. "I climbed the pole and cut them down. I believe there were eight altogether, two on four poles, and I wonder if the others were saved as well."

In 2006, Bethel Woods—Center for the Arts opened its doors. Adjacent property features a 7,500-square-foot stage, a 4,800-seat summer pavilion with space on the lawn for an additional 12,000 music patrons, an outdoor 700-seat amphitheatre, and an interpretive and multi-purpose gallery situated on the plateau that was once the concession area for Woodstock 1969. The gallery, which opened in 2007, consists of approximately 4,500 square feet intended for community gatherings, lectures, receptions, meetings, and other events. The interpretive center, housed within, opened in the summer of 2008 and includes 10,000 square feet of exhibition space telling the story of the 1960s, the 1969 Woodstock Festival, its historical context, and its influence on American culture.

Whether Woodstock's legacy has been preserved in Bethel Woods is for visitors to decide. Woodstock co-creator Michael Lang has repeatedly stated that "Woodstock is not a place. It's a state of mind."

Through the journey that we [Brad and Joanne] have taken to bring *Woodstock: Peace, Music & Memories* to life, it was apparent that whoever said, "If you remember Woodstock, you weren't there" probably didn't attend the watershed event—and wishes they had. It became evident that through every person and story that we've been privileged to have had shared with us, the music, mud, and enduring life lessons that played out for those days on Yasgur's farm in August of 1969 certainly do live on.

Photo by James Riley

Bethel Woods at night.

An aerial view from behind the stage at Woodstock.

Assuming the Mudra pose.

Woodstock is not a place. It's a state of mind.

Chapter 7

THEN AND NOW

Photos courtesy James Riley

Traveling along West Shore Road toward the Woodstock festival site.

It's been 40 years since the Woodstock Music and Arts Festival was held in Bethel, New York, and just as everywhere, change has taken place over time.

The El Monaco Hotel in White Lake, headquarters for Woodstock promoters and crew, was sold by Elliot Tiber soon after the concert. It continued to operate as a motel and restaurant until 2004, when it was demolished. A clock tower now sits on that corner, welcoming visitors to Bethel.

The Holiday Inn in Liberty, which served as a meeting place and housed many of the performers, is no longer operating, though the building still exists, and little remains of Grossinger's small airport. Vassmer's General Store in Kauneonga Lake later housed the Bethel Woodstock Museum. Known for passing out peanut butter and jelly sandwiches to hundreds of concert-goers in 1969, the store and museum closed their doors in 2004, and the Woodstock site is now part of Bethel Woods.

The area remains the rural farming area it was in 1969, and traveling down 17B or Hurd Road, one can only imagine what it looked like then—the crowds and the campers, the overflowing concert bowl, and the lake filled with people. Through the pictures in this chapter, we'd like to show you locations as they are today and provide you a glimpse back to those very same places on that weekend so long ago.

Using a keen eye, knowledge of the area, and some determination, Bethel local James Riley took his camera, love for the legacy of Woodstock '69, and photos from Woodstock—Peace, Music & Memories taken at the time of Woodstock, and set out in late 2008 to find and photograph these locations as they are today. Unlike so many locations that become unrecognizable after four decades, the Woodstock festival grounds and surrounding area, though enjoying a period of renewed growth and development, remain very similar today to what they looked like in August 1969.

Traveling along West Shore Road toward the Woodstock festival site.

Photos courtesy James Riley

Photo by Lee Levin-Friend

Route 17B toward Bethel, New York.

Photo courtesy James Riley

Photo courtesy Gary Geyer

The waterfall down the road from Forsythia Cove, 1969.

Photo courtesy James Riley

Waterfall, today.

Photo courtesy Gary Geyer

Forsythia Cove, 1969.

Photo courtesy James Riley

Forsythia Cove, today.

Photo by Randy Sheets

Security area and medical tent area, 1969.

Photo courtesy James Riley

Security area and medical tent area today.

Photo by John De Lorenzo

Pucky's (peat moss-filled) Pond, 1969.

Photo courtesy James Riley

Pucky's (peat moss-filled) Pond today.

Photo by Lee Levin-Friend

The crest of the concert hill, 1969.

Photo courtesy James Riley

The crest of the concert hill today.

Photo by Lynn Spencer

Looking down toward the stage, 1969.

Photo courtesy James Riley

Looking down toward the stage today.

Photo by John De Lorenzo

View from the main camping area toward the concert hill, 1969.

Photo courtesy James Riley

View from the main camping area toward the concert hill today.

View from the corner of Hurd Road and West Shore Road up the concert hill, 1969.

View from the corner of Hurd Road and West Shore Road up the concert hill today.

Happy Avenue.

The field from the stage area towards concession stands plateau.

Photo by Barry Smith

Vassmer's General Store (Kauneonga Lake), 2008, has new owners.

Photo by Barry Smith

West Shore Road behind stage area.

Photo by Barry Smith

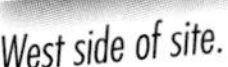

West side of site.

West Shore Road where the bridge crossed from the stage to the performer's area.

Photo by Barry Smith

Chapter 8

COLLECTING WOODSTOCK

Unlike the branding and mass merchandising of events that we see today, Woodstock 1969 did not have official merchandise that could be purchased as souvenirs. Other than an official festival program that arrived at the site at the end of the festival due to snarled traffic, other Woodstock-related items were either promotional, such as posters; functional, such as tickets; or crew apparel related to the Woodstock motion picture, which appeared in theaters a year following the festival.

For the next few decades following Woodstock, collecting artifacts was the domain of classic rock enthusiasts. With the advent of the internet, online auction houses like eBay, and two anniversary concerts, interest in collecting items original to the festival or related to it has continued to grow in popularity. Whether as an investment or for the joy of owning a piece of history, Woodstock collectibles enjoy values ranging from a few dollars to a few thousand dollars. Though money has become the antithesis of Woodstock, the current values shown in the following collectibles pale compared to the joy that having a piece of Woodstock holds for those collecting enthusiasts.

Woodstock Tickets

Courtesy Heritage Auction Galleries

Original single-day advanced sale tickets, $7 face value

Single ***$35***
Three-day set ***$100***

Original single-day gate tickets, $8 face value

Single ***$25***
Three-day set ***$80***

Original three-day advance sale passes, $18 face value.. ***$150***

Original three-day gate passes, $24 face value.............. ***$100***

Mounted single-day ticket displays........................... ***$35-$50***

Sotheby's Woodstock Memories mounted three-day pass ***$75***

Do you have original or second printing tickets?

Most, if not all, $7 face value single-day tickets are real. Most, if not all, $18 face value three-day advance sale passes are real. It can be difficult to tell as post-Woodstock tickets were printed with the original plates.

With $8 face value single-day tickets and $24 face value three-day gate tickets, the newer and crisper the ticket, the less chance that it is original. Watch out for very crisp looking orange and green tickets. The more faded the better.

Original Albums From Woodstock Performers

JOAN BAEZ

1969 David's Album

Vanguard VSD-79308 .... ***$12***

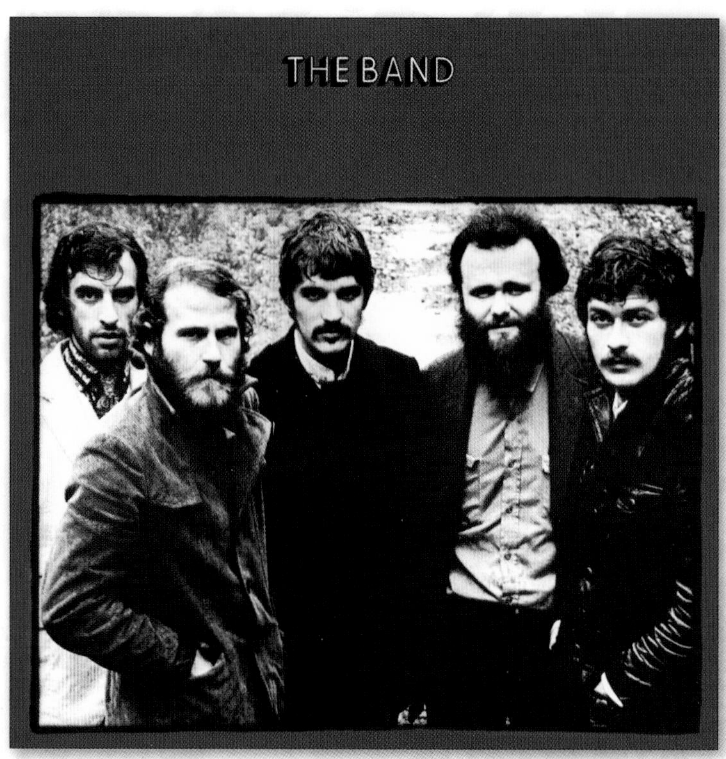

THE BAND

1969—The Band

Capitol STAO-132, lime green label................................ ***$15***

All values listed here, based on near mint (NM) condition, are from the fifth edition of *Goldmine Record Album Price Guide* and the fifth edition of the *Goldmine Standard Catalog of American Records 1950-1975*.

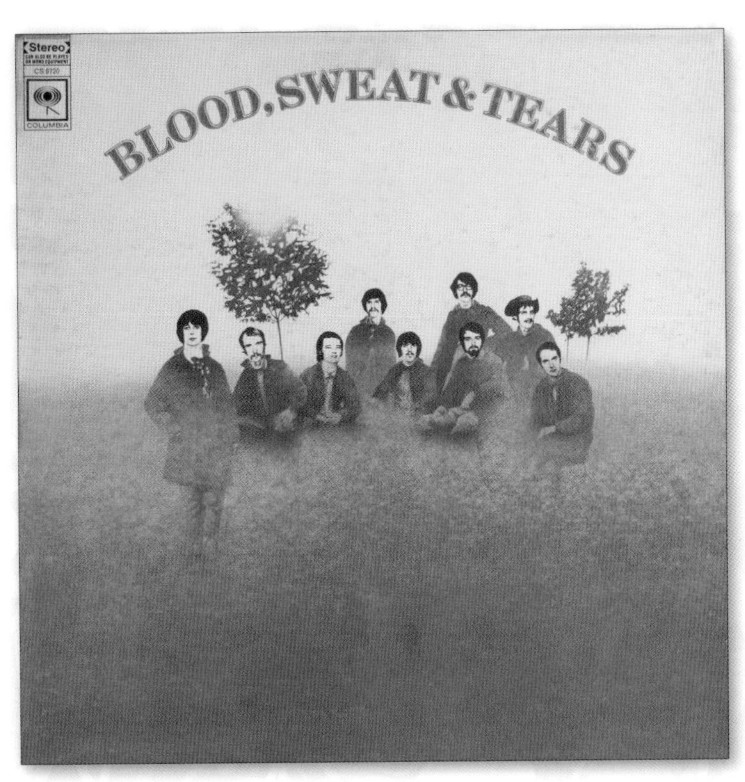

BLOOD, SWEAT AND TEARS
Blood Sweat and Tears 1969

Columbia CS 9720 .... ***$15***

THE PAUL BUTTERFIELD BLUES BAND
Keep On Moving 1969

Elektra EKS-74053, red label with large stylized "E" ***$20***

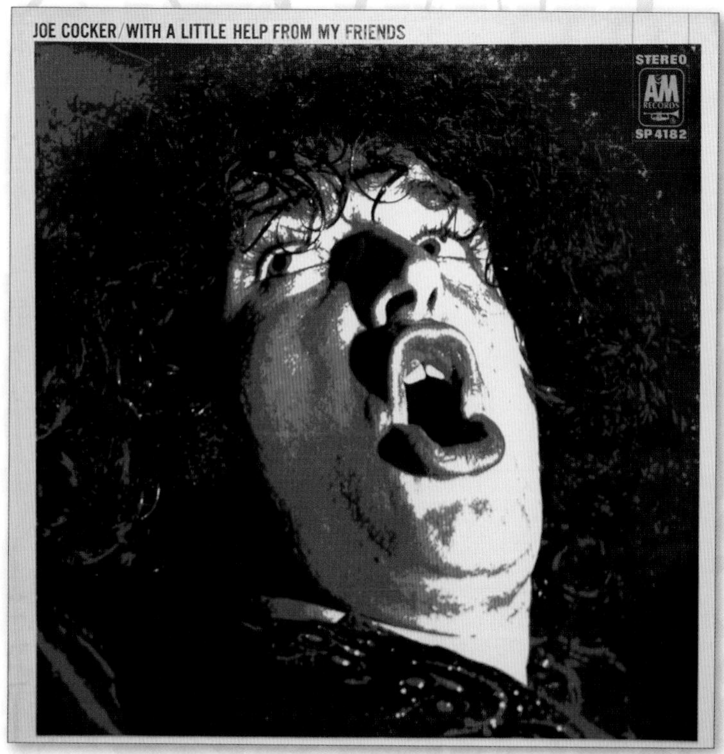

CANNED HEAT
Living the Blues 1968

Liberty LST-27200 [(2)] ***$25***

JOE COCKER
With A Little Help From My Friends 1969

A&M SP-4182, brown label ***$12***

COUNTRY JOE MCDONALD & THE FISH
Together 1968

Vanguard VSD-79277 .... ***$20***

CREEDENCE CLEARWATER REVIVAL
Green River 1969

Fantasy F-8393, dark blue label ***$15***
F-8393 [DJ].. ***$80***

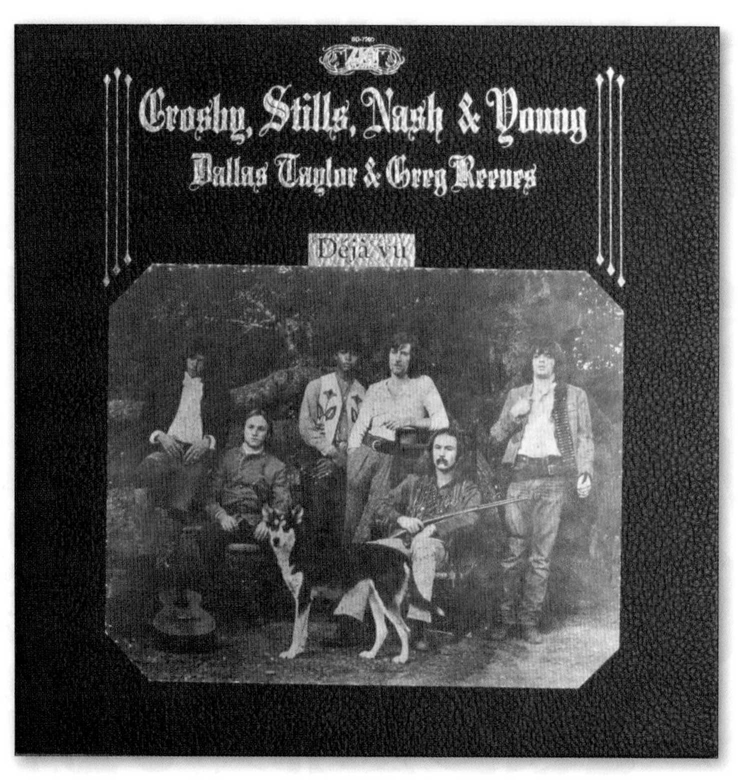

CROSBY, STILLS, NASH & YOUNG

Deja Vue 1970

Atlantic 7200 [M], white label promo ***$150***
SD 7200, pasted-on front cover must still be intact ***$15***
SD 7200 [DJ], white label stereo promo ***$60***

GRATEFUL DEAD

1969 Aoxomoxoa

Warner Bros. WS 1790, green label with "W7" logo **$30**

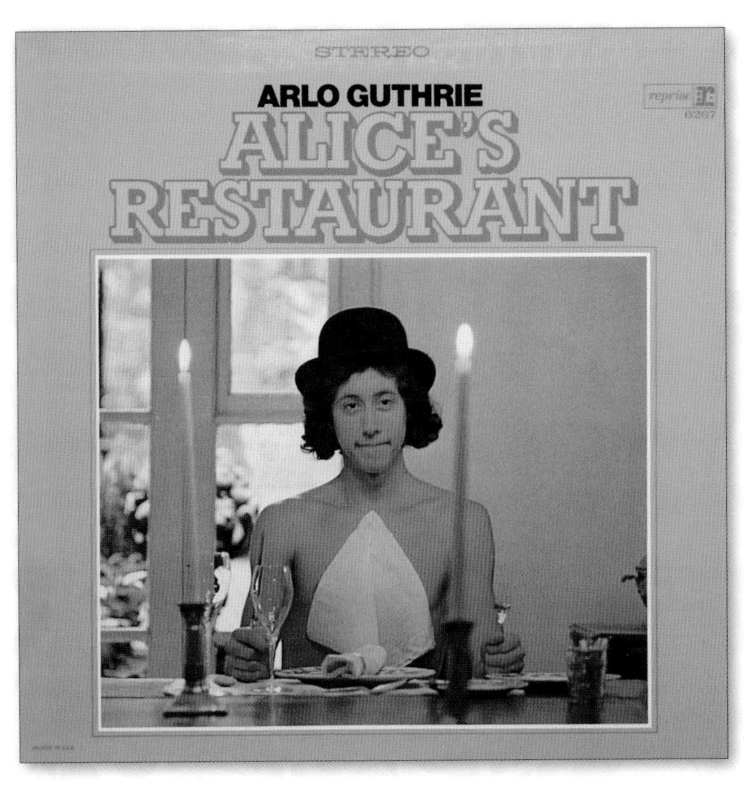

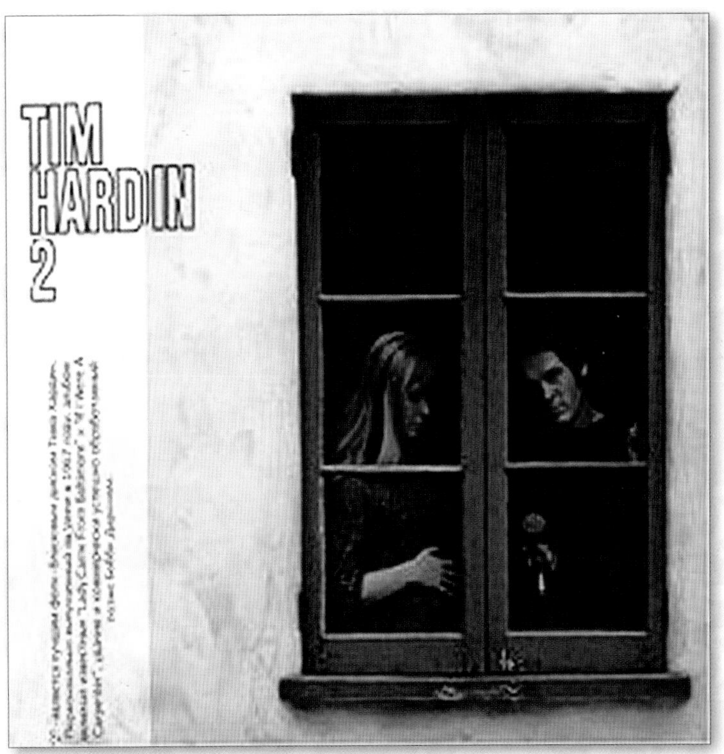

ARLO GUTHRIE

Alice's Restaurant 1967

Reprise R 6267 [M], pink, green, and gold label.............. ***$15***

TIM HARDIN

1967 Tim Hardin 2

Verve Forecast FTS-3022 .... ***$25***

RICHIE HAVENS

Mixed Bag 1967

MGM SE-4698 .... ***$15***

Stonehenge—1968

Stormy Forest SF 6001 .... ***$15***

KEEF HARTLEY

Halfbreed 1969

Deram Des 18024 .... ***$15***

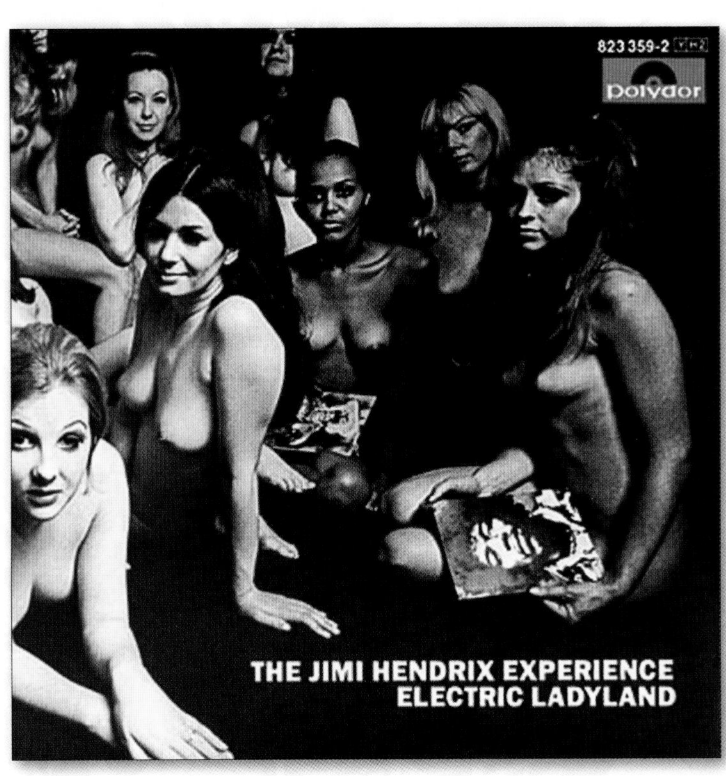

JIMI HENDRIX

1968 Electric Ladyland

Reprise RS 6261 [S] with "W7" and "r:" logos on two-tone orange label ***$25***

JIMI HENDRIX

Are You Experienced? 1967

R 6261 [M] ***$200***

THE INCREDIBLE STRING BAND

Wee Tam/Big Huge 1968

Elektra EKS-74036, brown label ***$20***

JANIS JOPLIN

I Got Dem Ol' Kozmic Blues Again Mama 1969

Columbia KSD 9913, "360 sound stereo" on label........... ***$20***

BIG BROTHER AND THE HOLDING COMPANY

Cheap Thrills 1968

Columbia KCL 2900 [M], red label stock copy has been confirmed ***$300***

KCS 9700 [M], white label "Special Mono Radio Station Copy" with stereo number ***$100***

KCS 9700 [S], red "360 Sound" label ***$25***

Pearl 1971

KC-30322 .... ***$15***

THE JEFFERSON AIRPLANE

Volunteers 1969

RCA Victor LSP-4238, orange label ***$12***

Surrealistic Pillow 1967

LPM-3766 [M] ***$60***

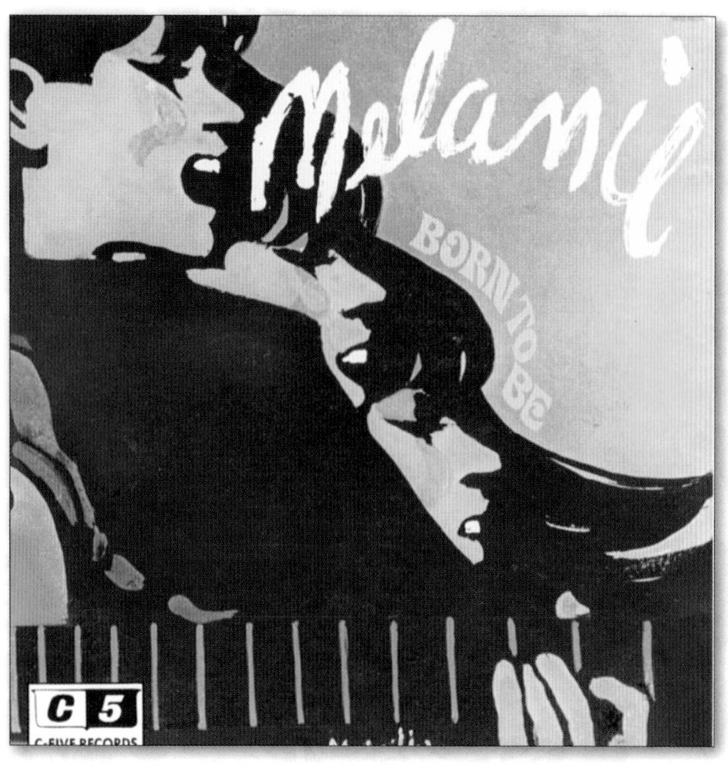

MELANIE

Born to Be 1968

Buddah BDS-5024 .... ***$15***

MOUNTAIN

Mountain 1969

Windfall 4500 .... ***$15***

SANTANA

Santana 1969

Columbia CS 9781, "360 Sound" on label...................... ***$15***

SWEETWATER

Sweetwater 1968

Reprise RS 6313.. ***$15***

JOHN SEBASTIAN—THE LOVIN' SPOONFUL

Do You Believe In Magic 1965

Kama Sutra KLPS-8050 [S]... ***$30***

SLY AND THE FAMILY STONE

Stand 1969

EPIC BN 26456.. ***$15***

BERT SOMMER

Inside Bert Sommer 1969

No established value

TEN YEARS AFTER

SSSH (Ten Years After) 1969

Deram Des 18029.. ***$15***

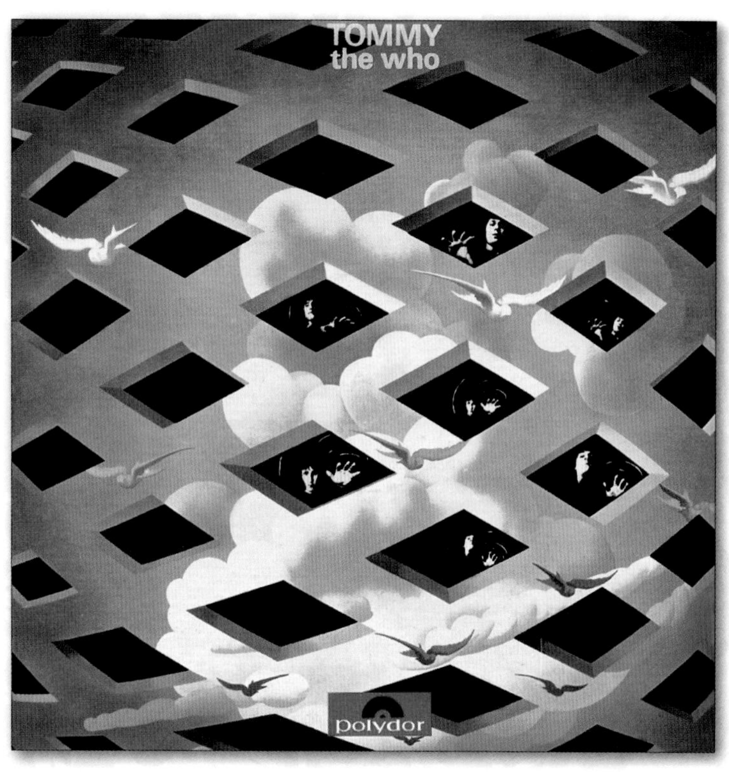

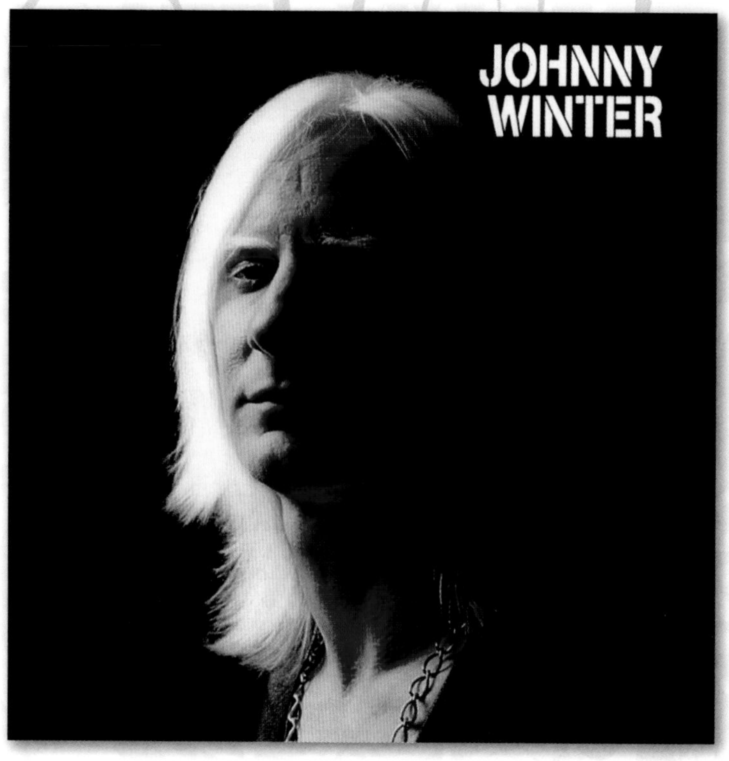

THE WHO
Tommy 1969

Decca DXSW 7205 [(2) DJ], white label promo ***$200***
DXSW 7205 [(2)], with booklet ***$40***

JOHNNY WINTER
Johnny Winter 1969

Columbia CS 9826, "360 Sound" on label...................... ***$20***

Original Compilation Albums and Related Artists

WOODSTOCK

3-LP set, Cotillion 1970

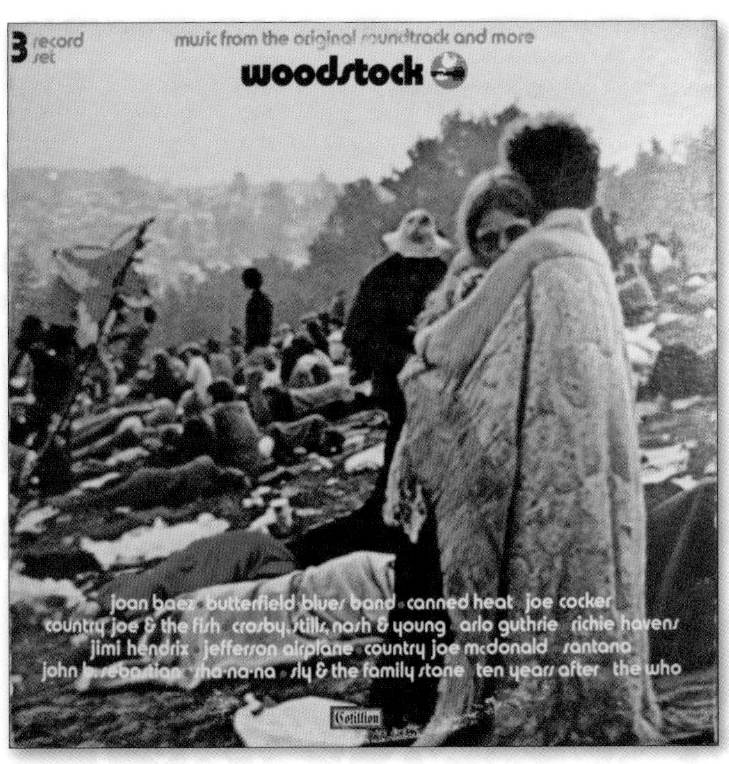

Original Woodstock 3-LP set. SD 3-500 on Original Cotillion Label. The vinyl is the thicker, more inflexible version associated with true first pressings. The address found on these Cotillion/ Atlantic Record labels, "1841 Broadway," also supports it as a first pressing issue. This 1970 first pressing also came with the wonderful pale blue labels shown in photos, which only came out in the 1970 editions. ***$20***

JIMI HENDRIX
Live at Woodstock 1999

Experience Hendrix/MCA 11987 [(3)]............................ ***$30***

JONI MITCHELL
Ladies of the Canyon 1970

Reprise RS 6376 with "W7" and "r:" logos on two-tone orange label.. ***$20***

RAVI SHANKAR

At the Woodstock Festival

World Pacific ST-21467 .... ***$15***

WOODSTOCK TWO

1971 N/A

Cotillion—SD 2-400 [(2)] **$20**

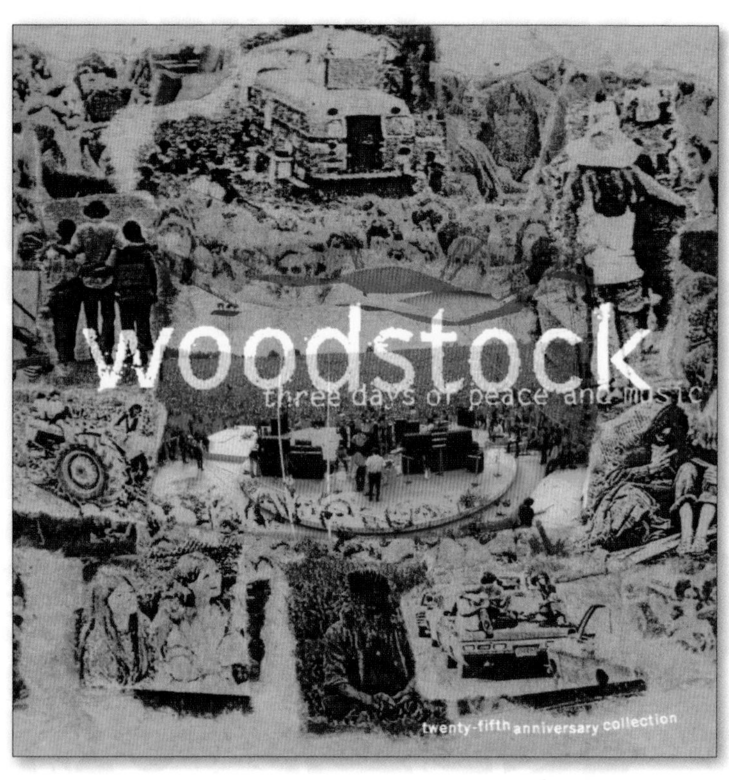

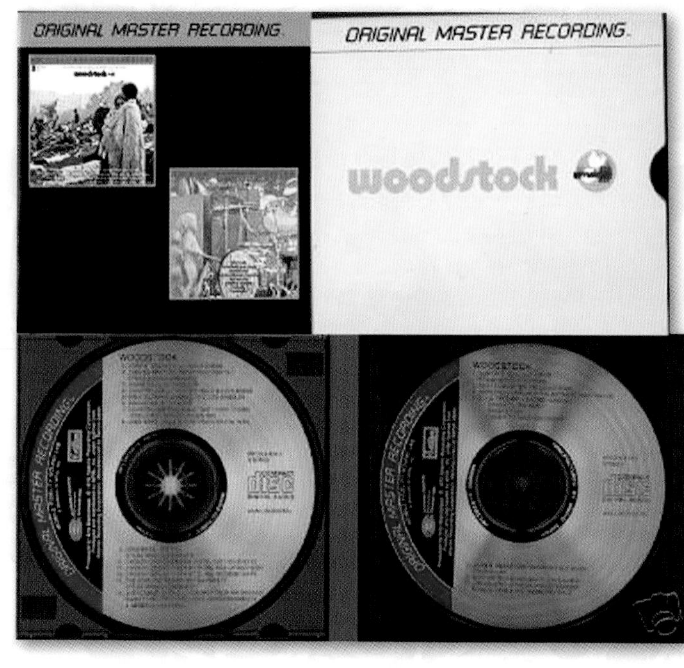

WOODSTOCK:
3 DAYS OF PEACE AND MUSIC

4-disc box set

Atlantic USA 1994 .... ***$25 (eBay)***

WOODSTOCK

MFSL 4-CD set

Contains an outer box with a pullout inner box holding two tri-fold LP packages (one containing two LPs and one containing three LPs) and a companion book documenting the event. ***$650 (eBay)***

Limited Edition MFSL 4-CD set .... ***$200 (eBay)***

Woodstock Posters

Original David Byrd Wallkill poster ***$150***

Heritage Auction Galleries

Original Woodstock dove on guitar poster, White Lake shown as location. *ArtRock Online* ***$2,250***

Original Woodstock dove on guitar poster, Wallkill shown as location. **$1,500**

Second printing, 1989 ArtRock Woodstock Dove on Guitar lithographs. *ArtRock Online*

Unsigned **$50**
Signed Grace Slick.. **$225**

Multiple signatures (Arnold Skolnick, Grace Slick, Country Joe, Carlos Santana, Wavy Gravy, Richie Havens) **$250**
1994-1999 Woodstock poster replicas **$20**

Do you have an original?

Original posters come in two sizes, 18" x 24" and 32" x 24". They were printed on either a heavier cardstock or on very thin paper to plaster on walls and billboards. If the poster looks new or is shiny poster paper, it is not original.

Many originals have a thin white border around them and have the printing company stamped on the reverse. If a poster has a white border with a larger border on the bottom, it is a second printing. If the color is orange and not red, and the details for camping, etc., only have the header "crafters bizarre," etc., with no text underneath, it is not original.

Courtesy Heritage Auction Galleries

Original Woodstock Motion Picture Poster...................... **$150**

Reprint of Woodstock Motion Picture Poster...................... **$20**

Woodstock Commemorative Posters

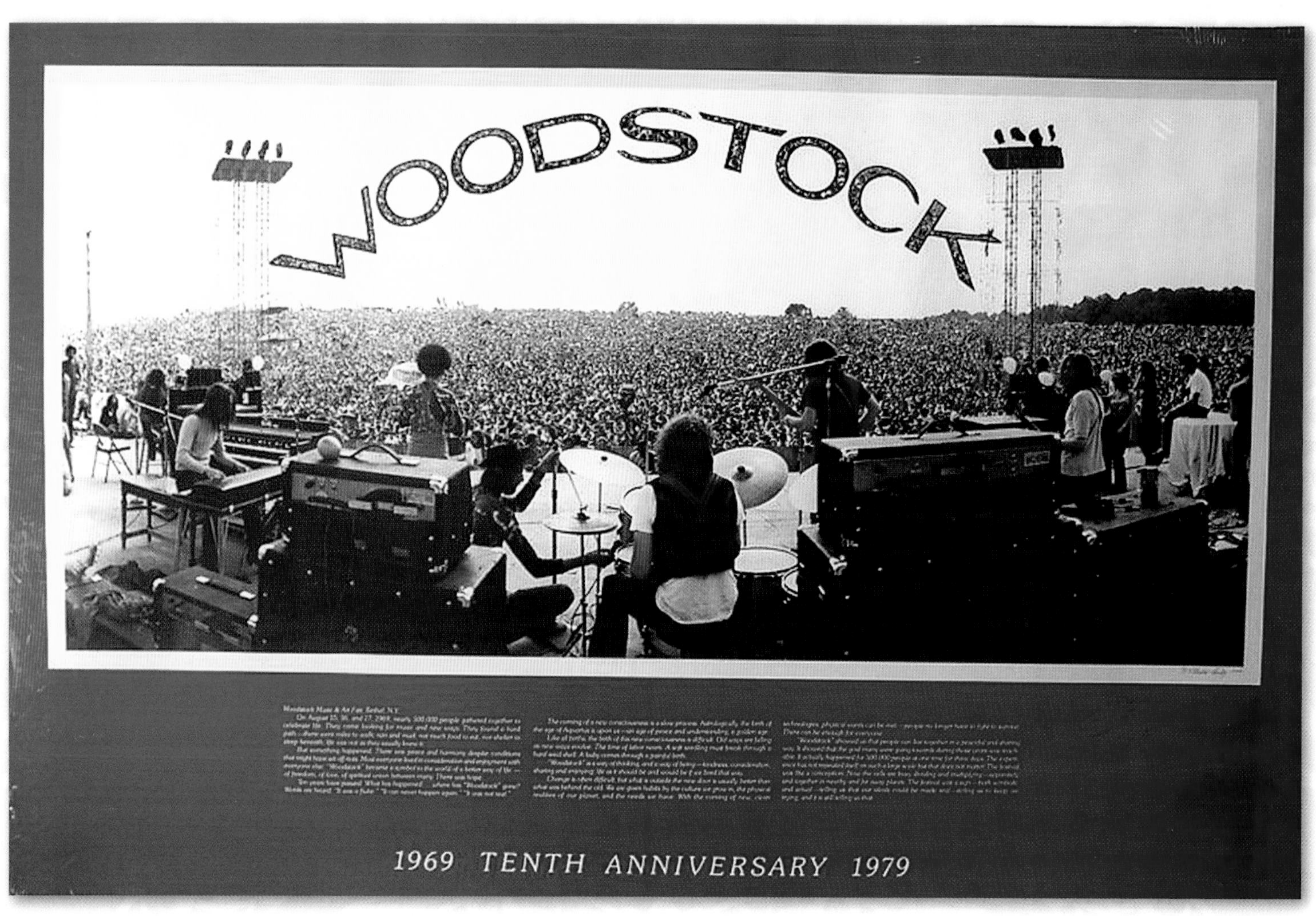

Elliott Landy ***$25***

WOODSTOCK

MUSIC & ART FAIR

PRESENTS AN

AQUARIAN EXPOSITION

IN WHITE LAKE, N.Y.

Jimi Hendrix

Grateful Dead

Janis Joplin

★ ★ ★

3 Days of Peace & Music

AUGUST 1969

★ ★ ★

Music Starts at 4:00 pm on Fri. and 1:00 pm Sat. & Sun.

Friday 15th	Saturday 16th	Sunday 17th
Joan Baez	Canned Heat	The Band
Arlo Guthrie	Creedence Clearwater	Jeff Beck Group
Richie Havens	Grateful Dead	Blood, Sweat & Tears
Sly and The Family Stone	Janis Joplin	Joe Cocker
Tim Hardin	Jefferson Airplane	Crosby Stills & Nash
Nick Benes	Santana	Jimi Hendrix
Sweetwater	The Who	Iron Butterfly
	Jack Harrison	Ten Years After
		Jonny Winter

★ ★ ★ ★ ★ ★

HUNDREDS OF ACRES TO ROAM ON

WOODSTOCK

MUSIC AND ARTS FAIR

JIMI HENDRIX

JANIS JOPLIN

AUGUST 15-16-17 - 1969

THREE DAY PEACE AND MUSIC FESTIVAL

★ FRIDAY THE 15th - Joan Baez, Arlo Guthrie, Richie Havens, Sly & The Family Stone, Tim Hardin, Nick Benes, Sha Na Na

★ SATURDAY THE 16th - Canned Heat, Creedence Clearwater, Melanie, Grateful Dead, Janis Joplin Jefferson Airplane, Incredible String Band, Santana The Who, Paul Butterfield, Keef Hartley

★ SUNDAY THE 17th - The Band, Crosby Stills Nash and Young, Ten Years After, Blood Sweat & Tears Joe Cocker, Jimi Hendrix, Mountain, Keef Hartley

AQUARIAN EXPOSITION

WHITE LAKE, NEW YORK

Post-Woodstock posters ***$15***

Books About Woodstock

All values vary based on new and used status (check Amazon.com).

The Age of Rock 2; Jonathan Eisen, Random House, New York, 1970

Aquarius Uprising; Robert Santelli, Delta Publishing, 1980, ISBN: 0-0440-50956-4

Barefoot in Babylon; John Spitz, WW Norton & Co., 1989, 515 pp., ISBN: 0-393-30644-5 (pbk)

Festival! The Book of American Music Celebrations; Jerry Hopkins (pictures by Jim Marshall and Baron Wolman), Collier/Macmillan Books, 1970, 191 pp.

I Want To Take You Higher—The Psychedelic Era 1965 1969 (The Rock and Roll Hall of Fame and Museum), edited by James Henke and Parke Puterbaugh, essays by Charles Perry and Barry Miles, Chronicle Books ISBN: 0-8118-V-8 (pbk), ISBN:0-8118-1725-3 (hc)

Knock On Woodstock; Elliot Tiber, Festival Books, 1994, 267 pp., ISBN: 0-9641806-1-8

The 60s; Blake Bailey, 1992

The Sixties; Lynda Rosen Obst and Robert Kingsbury, Random House/Rolling Stone, 1977, 317 pp. ISBN: 0-394-40687-1 ISBN: 0- 394-73239-1(pbk.)

The Story of Rock: Smash Hits and Superstars; Alan Dister, Discoveries, Harry N. Abrams, Inc., Publishers, 1992, ISBN 0-8109-2831-0 (pbk)

Taking Woodstock: A True Story of a Riot, a Concert, and a Life, Elliot Tiber with Tom Monte; Square One Publishers, 2007, 224 pp, IBSN-10 0757002935, ISBN-13: 978-0757002939

30 Years of Peace & Music & Other Things; Artie Kornfeld (Kornfeld at Woodstock LLC— Washington, D.C.), 1999, 129 pp. ISBN:0-9674885-0-8 (pbk with enhanced CD)

20 Years of Rolling Stone - What A Long, Strange Trip It's Been; edited by Jann S. Wenner, Straight Arrow/Friendly Press, 1987, 464 pp., ISBN: 0-914919-10-5

Woodstock; Dale Bell, Michael Wiese Productions, 1999, ISBN: 0-94- 118871-X (pbk)

Woodstock Festival Remembered; Jean Young and Michael Lang, Ballantine Books, 1979, 178 pp., ISBN: 0-345-28003-2

Woodstock 1969 - The First Festival; Elliot Landy, Square Books, 1994, 144 pp., ISBN: 0-916290-74-3

Woodstock: The Oral History (book and cassettes); Joel Makower, Dolphin/Double Day, 1989, ISBN: 0-385-24716-8, ISBN: 0-385-24717-6(pbk)

Woodstock 69 - Summer Pop Festivals (A Photo Review); Joseph J. Sia, Scholastic Book Services, 1970, 128 pp., catalog number 1618

Woodstock Songs and Photos; Warner Brothers Music, 1970, 96 pp., catalog number 2071

Woodstock: The Summer of Our Lives; Joel Curry, 1989

Woodstock Two; Warner Brothers Music, 64 pp.

Woodstock Vision—The Spirit of a Generation; Elliot Landy, LandyVision, 1994, 128 pp., ISBN: 0-9625073-4-2 (pbk.)

Young Men With Unlimited Capital; Joel Rosenman, 1989

Woodstock Videos and DVDs

Values vary based on new and used status. Most are available through Amazon.com and eBay.

Creation of the 1969 Woodstock Music Festival—Birth of a Generation, Virtue Films, 1994, Westlake Video, 1995, Cat. No. WS 1969 (60 min.)

Janis—The Way She Was, A Film, MCA Home Video, 1974, Cat. No. 80080 (96 min.)

Jimi Hendrix at Woodstock, BMG Video, Japan, 1992, Cat. No. BVVP-1001 (55 min.)

Jimi Hendrix: The Movie, Warner Bros Home Video, 1973, Cat. No. 11267 (102 min.)

Woodstock, Warner Bros Home Video, Cat. Nos. 1015 and 1016 *(Some are packaged separately and titled* Woodstock I *and* Woodstock II*; others are packaged in a single two-tape slipcover. Catalog numbers are for the separated videos.)*

Woodstock Diaries; Direct Video Distribution Ltd., Cat. No. B000067A82

Woodstock—Directors Cut, Warner Bros. Home Video, Cat. No. 13549 (219 min.)

Woodstock—The Lost Performances, Warner Bros. Home Video, Cat. No. 12202 (69 min.)

Viva Santana, CMV Enterprises/CBS Music Video Enterprises, Cat. No. 19V 49007 (82 min.)

Woodstock Magazines

Values based on near mint condition (from eBay).

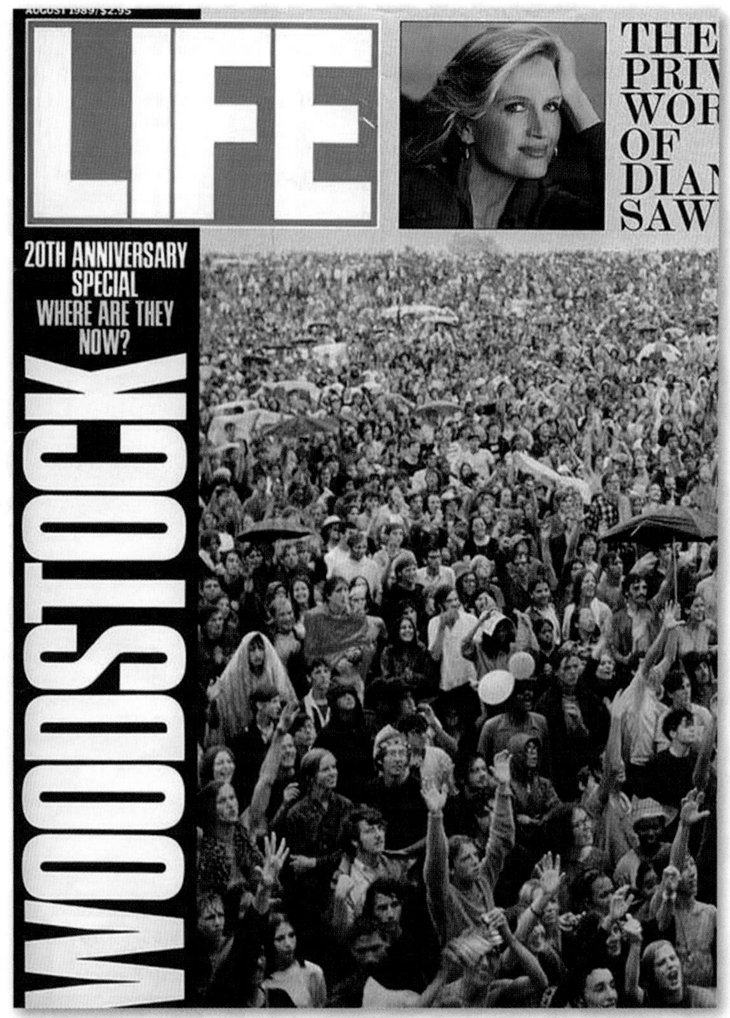

"20th Anniversary Special—Where Are They Now?"; Life, August 1989 .... **$10**

"Woodstock Music Festival," Special Edition; *Life,* 1969 .... **$61**

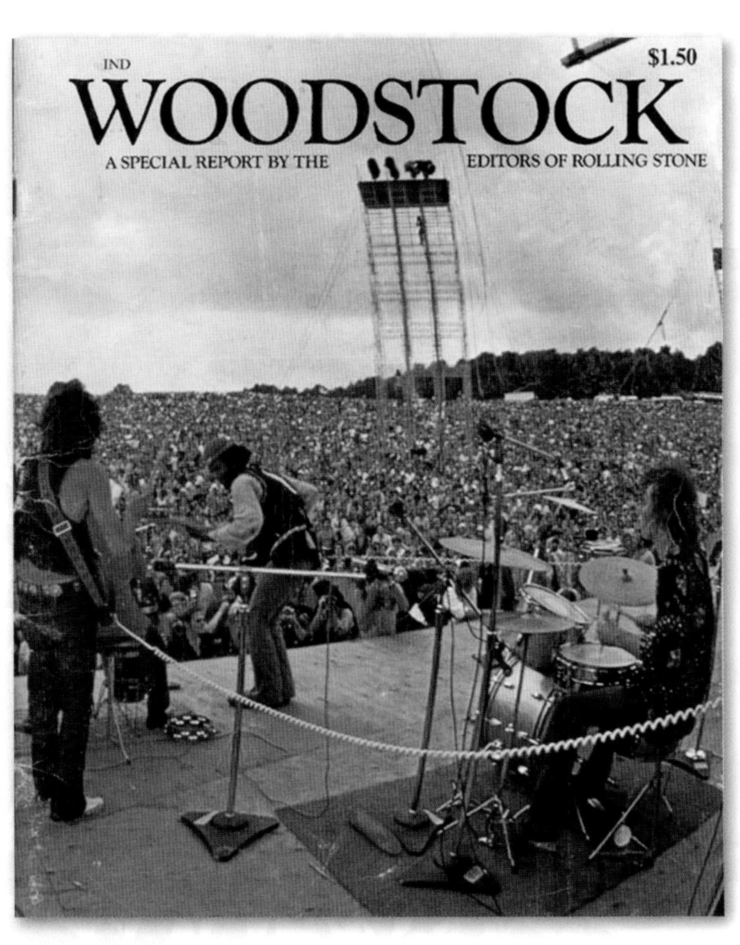

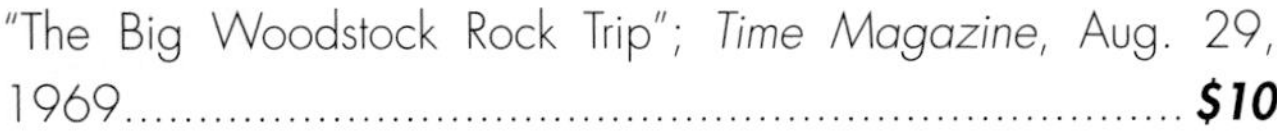
"The Big Woodstock Rock Trip"; *Time Magazine*, Aug. 29, 1969 .... ***$10***

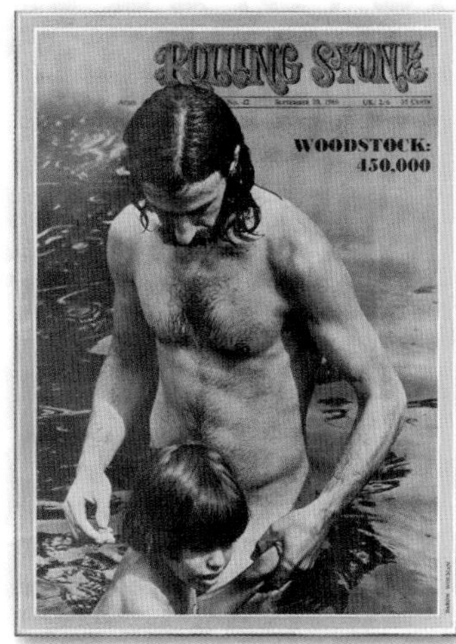

Rolling Stone #42, Sept. 20, 1969 .... ***$35***

Rolling Stone Special Edition ***$30***

"Woodstock—A 25th Commemorative"; special publication of *The Times-Herald-Record* 1994 .... ***$20***

Woodstock Ephemera

Heritage Auction Galleries

Original Official Woodstock program ***$130***

Official Woodstock program Reprint ***$45***

Do you have an original program?

Reprinted programs were made available in 1989 when purchasing the MFSL four-LP Woodstock soundtrack.

On the original program, the "f" in the word "of" sits directly in a sunflower bud. The first and last pages are thin, opaque, onion skin-like parchment. Almost every glossy image with a black background has little white dot imperfections. On the cover of an original program, the entire shaft of grass is visible. The tip of the grass is cut off on the cover of a reprint. In an original program, the Grateful Dead two-page spread has the same clarity on both pages; the pages look washed out in the reprint.

Official Woodstock motion picture program **$50**

Woodstock Wallkill advertisement **$25**

Heritage Auction Galleries

Original Woodstock brochure and order form................... **$70**

YASGUR FARMS DAIRY 34024
VISIT OUR FARM
QUALITY DAIRY PRODUCTS

WHITE LAKE 140 · MONTICELLO 2676 · JEFFERSONVILLE · BETHEL, N. Y.

SOLD TO

REC'D BY

Yasgur's Dairy receipt in Max Yasgur's writing ***$40***

Woodstock Motion Picture lobby card, signed by director Michael Wadleigh ***$35***

Woodstock—*Life*—Max Yasgur collector's card **$25**

SU VIVIE SURVIVE SURVI URVIVE SURVIVE SURVIVE S

We come to Hip City, USA. We no one of the largest cities in America (population 300,000 a growing all the time). We've got [illegible] traffic death, 15 miscarriages and a lot of mud. This is a d aster area.

Where we go from here depen on all of us. The people who promoted this festival have been overwl lme by their own creation. We can no longer remain passive consume / we have to begin to fend for ourselves

ACCESS -- The highways leading to the festival site are now blocked . Cars are being bturned back i an effort to clear highway 17B. The best thing you can do is to s y until the roads are cleared. If you decide to split and get stuck a team of repairmen is cruising the area and will free your car. n't leave your vehicle.

SANITATION -- Please stay off he roads. Garbage trucks need clear rights-of-way to pick up tras . Either burn your trash or dump it IN BAGS along the road (look r the stands with green bags hanging from them.) You MUST clean yo area to avoid a severe health hazard.

MEDICAL -- There are two majo medical stations. Minor stuff (cuts, bruises) can be taken care of at the SOUTH STATION near the Hog Farm, serious injuries will be trea d at the health trailer at the MAIN INTERSECTION, and drug freako s will be tended by the Hog Farm (red armband) people at the SOUTH AMPGROUND.

A planeload of doctors are eing airlifted from New York City, and a fleet of helicopters is bei g gathered to drop medical supplies.

y trained medical person t should report to the above medical centers.

Do not take any light blue lat acid and understand that taking strong dope at this time may ake you a drag in a survival situation.

Don't run naked in the hot n for any period of time. Water blisters are painful.

WATER -- Water is scarce. Sha e and conserve all water. Do not drink water unless it is crystal-cl ar. Check with festival and Hog Farm people before using any opera ing mains. New mains are being readied. We will announce their locati ns when they are made available. Blac k and white pipes are water pip s, don't use for walking or bridges. They break easily.

The lake is now a main sour e of water. Swimming will ruin the purification system -- think wic before taking a dip.

FOOD -- You should not be pig ish about your food and water. As with medicine, festival peop have promised that food will be airlifted into the area. The og Farm will continue to serve meals in the SOUTH AREA.

VOLUNTEERS -- Go to info. st d a main intersection

GENERAL HINTS - The thing t do is survive and share. Organize your own camping area so tha everyone makes it through uncomfortable t es ahead. Figure out what ou must do and the best ways to get it done.

PEOPLE WHO CANHELP DISTRIBU THIS LEAFLET SHOULD COME TO THE MOVEMENT CITY AREA IN TE SOUTH CAMPG UND.

R AD AND PAS ON

Original Woodstock survival flyer .... ***No established value***

Original Woodstock parking permit........ ***No established value***

Original Woodstock staff pass............... ***No established value***

STATE OF NEW YORK
DEPARTMENT OF MOTOR VEHICLES Used VEHICLE ORIGINAL CERTIFICATE OF SALE F047994

NAME AND ADDRESS OF DEALER: Kohlers Garage – Jeffersonville, N.Y. | YEAR: 1967 | TYPE: S/W | MAKE: Jeep
NAME AND ADDRESS OF PURCHASER: Woodstock Ventures Inc. 47 West 57th St. New York, N.Y. | WEIGHT: 2785 | MODEL: Jeepster | COLOR: Red | SEATING CAP.: 4
PLATE NO. OF PURCHASER: NA | INSPECTION CERT. NO.: 4344311 | DATE: 8/12/69 | INSPECTION STATION NO.: 3184 | SERIAL OR IDENTIFICATION NO.: 8705F1610466 | CYLS.: 6
SOURCE OF OWNERSHIP NAME AND ADDRESS: Otto Lowitz – Parksville, New York | LAST PLATE NO. OF VEHICLE: 9D6960 | DATE OF PURCHASE: 7/9/68
DLR. CERT. NO.: WN272 | DATE OF SALE: 8/12/69 | TEMP. CERT. OF REG. OR NO. OF DEALER PLATE LOANED: NA | ☒ GAS ☐ DIESEL ☐ ELECTRIC

I certify: Vehicle described above was sold to the purchaser on date indicated. At time of delivery the purchaser was entitled to register the vehicle. This vehicle complies with equipment requirements of the Commissioner's Regulations and such equipment was in condition and repair to render under normal use, satisfactory and adequate service upon the public highway at the time ... York State and Local Taxes due as a re...

CERTIFICATION OF RE...
I hereby certify that I have ... ☒ used ☐ demonstrator ve...
MV-50 (6/68)

STATE OF NEW YORK–DEPARTMENT OF MOTOR VEHICLES – AFFIDAVIT OF SALE OR TRANSFER

NOTE: 1. THIS FORM MUST BE ACCOMPANIED BY SUPPORTING DOCUMENTS.
2. NOT ACCEPTABLE WITH ANY CHANGES OR ALTERATIONS.
3. NOT TO BE USED BY A DEALER FOR SALE OF VEHICLES.

NAME OF SELLER: WOODSTOCK VENTURES, INC.
RESIDENCE ADDRESS: 47 W 57th ST.
CITY OR POST OFFICE: New York | COUNTY: N.Y. | STATE: N.Y. | ZIP CODE:
YEAR OF LAST REGISTRATION: 1968 | STATE OF LAST REGISTRATION: N.Y. | PLATE NO.: SC-1158 | VALIDATION NO.: UNK
NAME OF LAST REGISTRANT: Joseph Calandra
ADDRESS OF LAST REGISTRANT: Roscoe, N.Y.

VEHICLE DESCRIPTION
YEAR: 1967 | ☒ GAS ☐ ELECTRIC ☐ DIESEL
MAKE: Jeep
BODY TYPE: Jeep
VEHICLE IDENT. NO.: 8305C-213144
COLOR: Red
WEIGHT: 2440 LBS. | CYLS.: 6

PURCHASER: BEFORE PURCHASING, BE SURE THAT YOU KNOW OF ANY LIENS AGAINST THE VEHICLE.
NAME OF PURCHASER: Ken's Garage – Kenneth Van Loan
RESIDENCE ADDRESS: Kauneonga Lake | CITY OR POST OFFICE: N.Y.
COUNTY: Sullivan | STATE: N.Y. | ZIP CODE: 12749 | DATE OF PURCHASE: 10/1/69

VEHICLE INSPECTION DATA
DATE OF LAST INSPECTION: 8/12/69
INSP. CERTIFICATE NO.: 4344312
STATION NO.: 3184

PRINT IN INK OR TYPE ALL ENTRIES
MV-51 (10-67) AFFIDAVITS ON REVERSE SIDE MUST BE SIGNED BEFORE PERSON AUTHORIZED TO TAKE AFFIDAVITS. (SEE OTHER SIDE)

Original signed Woodstock receipts .... ***No established value***

Other Woodstock Collectibles

Woodstock motion picture promotion pinback.................... ***$15***

Woodstock paperweight containing piece of stone from original festival site .... ***No established value***

Photo courtesy PeaceFence.com

James Alexy (1969-1999), founder of PeaceFence.com.

Photo courtesy PeaceFence.com

Peacefence pendant, handcrafted from the original Woodstock fence by C. Alexy and Associates, Bethel, New York. ***$40***

Original Yasgur Farms milk bottles—Pint............................ ***$75***

Original Yasgur Farms milk bottles—Quart...................... ***$100***

PREMIER TALENT ASSOCIATES, INC. / 200 WEST 57TH STREET
New York, N.Y. 10019 • 757-4300

PREMIER TALENT ASSOCIATES INC. JUL 30 1969

AGREEMENT made this 27th day of JUNE, 19 69.

between NEW ACTION LTD. FURNISHING THE SERVICES OF THE WHO (hereinafter referred to as "ARTIST") and WOODSTOCK VENTURES INC. (hereinafter referred to as "PURCHASER").

THIS CONTRACT IS ... SUBJECT TO IMMIGRATION AND NATURALIZATION CLEARANCE.

It is mutually agreed between the parties as follows:

The PURCHASER hereby engages the ARTIST and the ARTIST hereby agrees to perform the engagement hereinafter provided, upon all of the terms and conditions herein set forth, including those hereof entitled "Addi- Terms and Conditions."

1. PLACE OF ENGAGEMENT AQUARIAN FESTIVAL GROUNDS
   Exact address WALLKILL, NEW YORK
2. DATE(s) OF ENGAGEMENT AUGUST 16 17, 1969
3. HOURS OF ENGAGEMENT ONE (1) ONE (1) HOUR SHOW. PLEASE ADVISE SHOW TIMES.
4. REHEARSAL(s) REPORT TIME 12 NOON.
5. FULL PRICE AGREED UPON: TWELVE THOUSAND FIVE HUNDRED DOLLARS FLAT ($12,500.00)

All payments shall be paid by certified check, money order, bank draft or cash as follows:

(a) $ 6,250.00 shall be paid by PURCHASER to and in the name of ARTIST'S agent, PREMIER TALENT ASSOCIATES, INC., not later than IMMEDIATELY;

(b) $ 6,250.00 shall be paid by PURCHASER to ARTIST not later than IN CASH ONLY PRIOR TO SHOW DAY OF ENGAGEMENT.;

(c) Additional payments, if any, shall be paid by PURCHASER to ARTIST not later than

PURCHASER shall first apply any and all receipts derived from the engagement hereis to the payments required hereunder: All payments shall be made in full without any deductions whatsoever.

6250 RR

6. SCALE OF ADMISSION

****ARTIST IS TO RECEIVE 100% STAR BILLING. ARTISTS ARE BILLED IN ALPHABETICAL ORDER.
THIS IS A FESTIVAL CONCEPT; THEREFORE PLACEMENT OF ACT IS AT THE DISCRETION OF PROMOTER.
FB:rr

Return all signed copies to agent:
Premier Talent Associates, Inc.

NEW ACTION LTD. FURNISHING THE SERVICES OF THE WHO
By

WOODSTOCK VENTURES INC. (PURCHASER)
By SIGN HERE → Michael Lang
Address: 513 A 6th AVENUE
N. Y. C.
Phone: (212) CH3-6260

THE ABOVE SIGNATURES CONFIRM THAT THE PARTIES HAVE READ AND APPROVE EACH AND ALL OF THE "ADDITIONAL TERMS AND CONDITIONS" SET FORTH ON THE REVERSE SIDE HEREOF.
PLEASE INITIAL BACK OF CONTRACT.

Lithograph contract for The Who to perform at Woodstock (bonus insert from The Who "Live at Leeds" LP)............................ ***$10***

Original Woodstock crew shirt...................................... ***$350***
Original Woodstock security shirt ***$250***

Mary-Lou Littleproud (author's wife) wears an authentic Woodstock security shirt at the 2003 Toronto Sars concert with 500,000 in attendance.. ***Priceless***

Courtesy Heritage Auction Galleries

Graham Nash's Woodstock t-shirt. This is Graham Nash's t-shirt from Woodstock, a personal souvenir from a career highlight. In very fine condition with mild wear and soiling.......... ***No established value***

Die-cast "Light" bus and gear from Sun Star Die-Cast America Inc., 2009.

The sphinx side of "Light" bus.

Photos courtesy Sun Star Die-Cast America Inc.

DIE-CAST WOODSTOCK "LIGHT" BUS

An exact replica of the Bob Hieronimus-painted VW "Light" bus, measuring 14" x 6" x 6", with removable musicians' gear, is available from Sun Star Models Development Ltd.

Artist Bob Hieronimus calls his art "symbolic" because all of his designs are part of a comprehensive message. According to the artist, a simplified symbolic interpretation of all five sides of the bus says there are advanced beings in the universe that are assisting earth's evolution toward cosmic consciousness. This bus carried the message of "serving others as we evolve."

On the front of the bus, cosmic vibration is portrayed in a galaxy of stars, a pair of wings (spirit), a circled cross related to the four builders of the universe (air, earth, fire, and water), a hand holding an Egyptian Sistrum, and a fish swallowing cosmic vibrations from the urn of Aquarius.

The eagle symbolizes the United States, which was established as a center of light (wisdom) to free humanity to serve the divine plan. The opened wings of the eagle shed "Light." The roof illustrates the balance of masculine and feminine energies. The red (masculine) and white (feminine) stripes from the American flag mimic the waves of Aquarius, and the 10 red flowers are symbols for the cycles of life and death.

The eagle side of die-cast "Light" bus.

The sphinx is spiritual conscious control (human head) over animal instincts (animal body). The mystery schools of the ancients (Egypt, India, Hebrews) taught the science of spirituality and how humanity can transform its physical consciousness into spiritual awareness.

The rear of the bus is about balancing feminine and masculine energies. On the left is fire (masculine, outgoing, electric), on the right is water (feminine, magnetic), which combine into the rising sun.

Sun Star Models Development Ltd. Is a manufacturer of diecast and plastic models for collectors worldwide. Models range from 1/12 to 1/43 scale with many working mechanisms such as wheels, steering, doors, hoods, and highly detailed motors and interiors, all packaged in attractive commercial boxes. The Light bus model retails for approximately $300 at hobby or model shops.

Rear view of the Woodstock "Light" bus from Sun Star Die-Cast America Inc., 2009.

Photo by Dr. Bob Hieronimus

The original "Light" bus. Artist Bob Hieronimus painted it with flowers and symbols representative of the time.

EPILOGUE

I believe what was most significant about Woodstock was that all these young people were coming from different parts of the country where their opposition to the war in Vietnam, their long hair, and tie-dyed clothes were frowned upon. At Woodstock they suddenly discovered that there were half a million people just like them, going along with where they were coming from. They created, what Abbie Hoffman later called, the Woodstock Nation, and that was very exciting.

When it became impossible for basic services to move in and out of the event, and it was declared a disaster area, the entire world's media was focused on us. It was our opportunity to show what we could do, so we pulled ourselves up by our collective bootstraps, and we were amazing together. I believe the universe was acting out these archetypes. I've puzzled over it for decades, and that's the best I can come up with.

I've recently attended some quite extraordinary events, and people can, and still do, get together for a weekend of peace, love, and music. I believe the true *Woodstock* is in everyone's hearts and consciousness—the caring, sharing, and reaching out to help each other through whatever life's storms may bring.

And to all those who shared that weekend with me so long ago, I say, "Hippies of the world, unite. We can still change the world through peace, love, and understanding."

Wavy Gravy
(telephone conversation with Joanne Hague on Oct. 2, 2008)

ABOUT THE AUTHORS

With a longtime interest in the socio-cultural history of the 1960s and a passion for the classic rock music of that era, Brad Littleproud of Toronto, Canada, and Joanne Hague of Blakely, Pennsylvania, were intrigued with the allure surrounding the fabled 1969 Woodstock festival.

They became members of the Woodstock Preservation Alliance, an organization founded to perpetuate the spirit of Woodstock and to preserve the site as an open field where all people would be welcome to celebrate peace, love, and music.

It was the compelling sense of these two people, who embraced that mission and evolved into an independent preservation entity. They led the cause for the historic preservation of an irreplaceable piece of global history and fought for the adherence to the best practices in preservation planning – efforts that spanned over two years and included local, state, and federal government/agencies. With few resources but a wealth of determination, it was shown that a few caring individuals can effect change, or at least persuade the powers that be to weigh their plans.

The Woodstock site will continue to have some resemblance to its original state for years to come and will allow visitors to experience an icon of a generation. Littleproud and Hague feel that they had some influence in protecting this parcel of peace, and for that, their battle was worth it.

Their work continues through the Woodstock Preservation Archives (www.woodstockpreservation.org), the most comprehensive and educational Woodstock '69 website on the Internet. It is the documented account of the historic preservation efforts of the original Woodstock site in Bethel, New York, and hosts the unique Woodstock Historian program, which provides students with the opportunity to receive firsthand information by corresponding directly with Woodstock veterans to help better understand what took place on that weekend 40 years ago.

Despite the fact that both Littleproud and Hague were too young to have attended the original festival in 1969, their work has transported them back in time to share Woodstock with half a million others.

MORE ABOUT MUSIC AND MAKING MEMORIES

Woodstock Revisted

50 Far Out, Groovy, Peace-Loving, Flashback-Inducing Stories From Those Who Were There

Edited by Susan Reynolds

Revel in the memories of Woodstock from the people who danced on the field, frolicked in the mud and rain, and grooved to the tunes and message of this festival forty years ago. This book chronicles the event through first person accounts and paints a mesmerizing and nostalgic portrait of America at the close of the tumultuous 1960's.

Item# Z3832 • $12.95

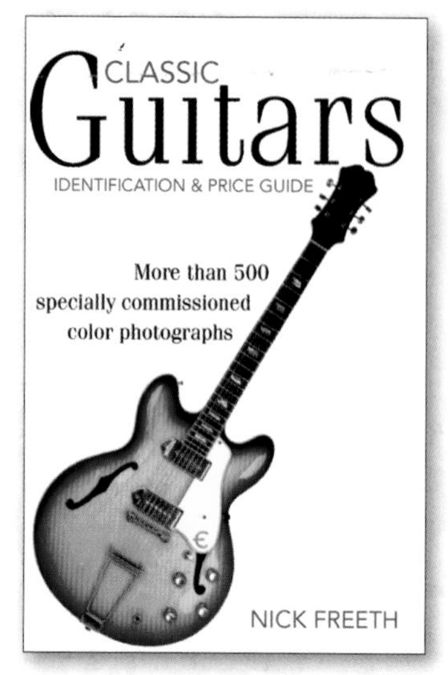

Classic Guitars

Identification and Price Guide

by Nick Freeth

Review brief histories, collector values and stunning color photos of 260 of the most famous brands of classic guitars

Softcover • 6 x 9 • 272 pages
750+ color photos
Item# Z0913 • $19.99

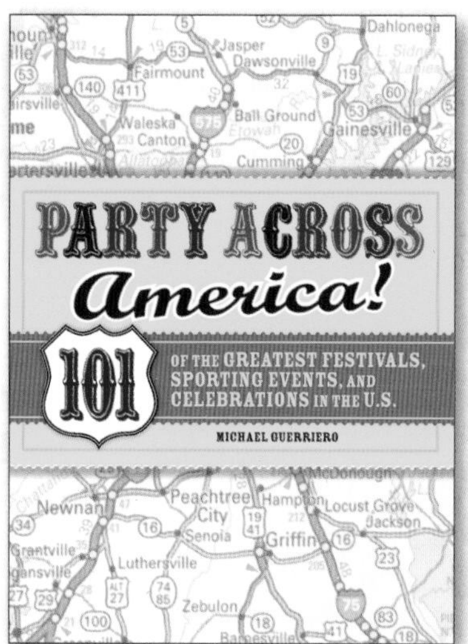

Party Across America!

101 of the Greatest Festivals, Sporting Events and Celebrations in the U.S.

by Michael Guerriero

Looking for a way to relive some of your carefree cool of yesteryear? Seeking ways to show your family, friends and even yourself the more intriguing parts of the country? This book gives you 101 ideas and opportunities to make new life-long memories, like rocking like a superstar in Tennessee at Bonnaroo.

Item# 1-59869-816-8 • $12.95

Goldmine® Fabulous Fifties with Elvis & Friends CD

From the Editors of Goldmine

CD-ROM

Before Santa, Canned Heat and Hendrix took the stage at Woodstock the pioneers of rock 'n' roll laid the ground work, and ushered in a sound and experience never before seen. This easy-to-search CD features 25 classic issues from the Goldmine magazine vault of vinyl history, featuring the legends including Elvis, Fats and Jerry Lee Lewis, among others. In addition, with the click of a mouse you'll gain access to an exclusive countdown to the 50 most valuable Elvis records.

Item# Z2979 • $19.99

Krause Publications, Offer **ACB9**
P.O. Box 5009
Iola, WI 54945-5009
www.krausebooks.com

Call 800-258-0929 8 a.m. - 5 p.m. to order direct from the publisher, or visit booksellers nationwide or antiques and hobby shops.

Please reference offer **ACB9** with all direct-to-publisher orders

Order directly from the publisher at
www.krausebooks.com